European Socialism and the Conflict in Central America

THE WASHINGTON PAPERS

. . . intended to meet the need for an authoritative, yet prompt, public appraisal of the major developments in world affairs.

President, CSIS: David M. Abshire

Series Editor: Walter Laqueur

Director of Publications: Nancy B. Eddy

Managing Editor: Donna R. Spitler

MANUSCRIPT SUBMISSION

The Washington Papers and Praeger Publishers welcome inquiries concerning manuscript submissions. Please include with your inquiry a curriculum vitae, synopsis, table of contents, and estimated manuscript length. Manuscripts must be between 120–200 double-spaced typed pages. All submissions will be peer reviewed. Submissions to *The Washington Papers* should be sent to *The Washington Papers*; The Center for Strategic and International Studies; 1800 K Street NW; Suite 400; Washington, DC 20006. Book proposals should be sent to Praeger Publishers; One Madison Avenue; New York NY 10010.

European Socialism and the Conflict in Central America

Eusebio M. Mujal-León

Foreword by Simon Serfaty

Published with The Center for
Strategic and International Studies
Washington, D.C.

PRAEGER

New York
Westport, Connecticut
London

F
1436.7
. M 85
1989

C

Library of Congress Cataloging-in-Publication Data

Mujal-León, Eusebio M., 1950–
    European socialism and the conflict in Central America / Eusebio
M. Mujal-León.
        p.   cm. – (Washington papers, ISSN 0278-937X ; 138)
    "Published with the Center for Strategic and International
Studies, Washington, D.C."
    Includes index.
    ISBN 0-275-93238-9 (alk. paper). – ISBN 0-275-93239-7 (pbk. :
alk. paper)
    1. Central America – Relations – Europe, Western.   2. Europe,
Western – Relations – Central America.   3. P.S.O.E. (Political party)
Influence.   4. Parti socialiste (France) – Influence.
5. Sozialdemokratische Partei Deutschlands – Influence.   6. Central
America – Politics and government – 1979–   7. Socialism – Central
America – History – 20th century.   I. Center for Strategic and
International Studies (Washington, D.C.)   II. Title.   III. Series.
F1436.7.M85   1989
303.4′82728′04 – dc 19   88-35952

The *Washington Papers* are written under the auspices of The Center
for Strategic and International Studies (CSIS) and published
with CSIS by Praeger Publishers. The views expressed in these papers
are those of the authors and not necessarily those of the Center.

Library of Congress Catalog Card Number: 88-35952
ISBN: 0-275-93238-9 (HB)
        0-275-93239-7 (PB)

First published in 1989

Praeger Publishers, One Madison Avenue, New York, NY 10010
A division of Greenwood Press, Inc.

Printed in the United States of America

∞

The paper used in this book complies with the Permanent
Paper Standard issued by the National Information Standards
Organization (Z39.48-1984).

10 9 8 7 6 5 4 3 2 1

Contents

Foreword

The postwar history of U.S.-European relations is a history of cooperation and discord. From Harry Truman through Ronald Reagan, the permanence of discord has caused each U.S. president to face an "Atlantic crisis" he could legitimately call his own, whether over the rearmament of Germany and the management of the Soviet threat, the organization of NATO and the credibility of the Western deterrent, the impact of the U.S. dollar on European economies as well as the European Community's impact on the U.S. economy, economic sanctions against the East, or burden sharing in the West. Yet, as a reflection of the enduring ties between the two sides of the Atlantic, never did the *déjà vu* of discord ever threaten truly to degenerate into the *jamais vu* of rupture.

Clashes of ambivalent interests outside of the NATO area proper have often been at the center of the sharpest interallied disputes: first, during the painful demise of Europe's empires, when the United States complained of European colonial policies that gave the West a bad name in the Third World; later when it was Europe's turn to criticize U.S. policies in Southeast Asia, the Caribbean and South America, Southern Africa, and the Middle East and the Gulf—policies now said to compromise the presence and influence of the West in some vital areas of the Third World.

The periodicity of these bouts of discord alone should have taught that Atlantic tensions do not result from any specific political alignments in Europe (whether Gaullist in the 1960s or Eurocommunist in the 1970s) or from any single president of the United States (whether of an allegedly liberal or conservative political persuasion). Yet, as the 1980s began, it was feared that the nearly simultaneous emergence in the United States and some European countries of new mandarins with two fundamentally contradictory perspectives on Third World issues would create difficult and even irreconcilable confrontations among the allies.

On the projected front line of such confrontations there was, perhaps first and foremost, Central America. There, Europe's Socialist and Social Democratic parties showed a marked predilection for "unbridled optimism and intense involvement," which conservative parties on the Continent were themselves reluctant to criticize too overtly. Not surprisingly, early attempts by the Reagan administration to gain a measure of benign support from the European allies for U.S. policies in that region remained, therefore, totally unsuccessful. "I support the revolt of these people," said François Mitterrand instead, in early 1982. "If that does not please the United States, and it clearly does not, it is just too bad."

This early phase of transatlantic tensions did not last long, however; it quickly gave way to a period described in the pages that follow as one of "modified perspectives and reduced activism." In this volume, Professor Eusebio Mujal-León superbly reviews, analyzes, and discusses the evolving views of European socialism toward the conflict in Central America. But the implications of his work go far beyond the narrow scope of this sole area of discord among the allies. Instead, implications can be found for the whole landscape of Atlantic relations.

Thus, written into this volume is a lesson that teaches how a measure of indifference to, and tolerance for, European criticism of U.S. policies in the Third World can serve

U.S. and Atlantic interests well. As initial disagreements were not turned by the Reagan administration into tests of Atlantic cohesion or solidarity in 1981-1982, Europe's criticism of U.S. policies decreased in 1982-1986. Specifically with regard to Central America, Europe's romance with revolutions faded, because these had not kept all their promises (as in Nicaragua) or because their continued dependence on the Soviet Union (as in Cuba) became all the more questionable as the Soviet image was sharply devalued on all sides of the political spectrum in Europe. Thus able to overcome an admittedly difficult and conflictual start, the Reagan administration was able to mute discord over such other questions as Grenada (where U.S. intervention caused limited and short-lived criticism) and El Salvador (where José Napoleón Duarte received increasing support following the elections of April 1984) – questions that, under different circumstances, would have been the focus of bitter disputes with potentially serious consequences on the general tenure of allied relations.

Simultaneously, the Reagan administration was displaying a similar measure of tolerance over policy differences involving other areas of the Third World (including the Middle East and the Gulf), while it focused its attention on vital security issues involving the military balance in Europe. Accordingly, the tensions that had been inherited from the previous decade, which peaked over issues of East-West trade after the 1982 Versailles Summit, were overcome. In May 1983, the summit that was held in Williamsburg showed a degree of allied unity that had not been seen in a generation. With the U.S. economy well into the first year of its longest peacetime recovery, the promises of U.S. leadership were renewed – even for Socialist parties that found in the U.S. model much that was worth emulating, often at the cost of some of their most entrenched economic and social dogmas. And with the growing perception of an incompetent but dangerous Soviet regime spreading during the waning years and immediate aftermath of the Brezhnev regime (peaking with the Soviet walkout from the arms control negotiations in Geneva in November 1983), the renewal of U.S. power was applauded—even for parts of the European Left whose visceral objection to the use of force in the Third World was accordingly reappraised.

"At the end of the 1980s," concludes Professor Eusebio Mujal-León in this much-needed study, "Central America is no longer on the front line of divergences" between the United States and the European Socialists. To be sure, such a happy ending might not endure: since 1986, the author also argues, there has been "renewed activism and intensified engagement." But such conclusions need not be limited solely to the question of Atlantic discord and cooperation in Central America.

With a new and vigorous leadership at the helm, the Soviet Union has launched a diplomatic offensive in Europe whose scope, pace, and intensity are all the more significant as the U.S.-Soviet summit held at Reykjavik in October 1986, together with the unprecedented stock market crash of October 1987, has raised new apprehensions in Europe about the reliability of U.S. leadership in preserving Europe's security and prosperity. This volume provides a critical understanding of and insight into the many nuances that have shaped, and continue to shape, the changing perspectives and activities of the major European Socialist and Social Democratic parties regarding Central America. It thereby helps the reader understand how such activism and engagement can be managed most effectively there and elsewhere, and whether any resulting improvement in U.S.-European relations over any recurring area of discord can be sustained over and beyond that area during the coming years.

Simon Serfaty
Executive Director
The Johns Hopkins Foreign Policy Institute
Washington, D.C.

February 1989

About the Author

Eusebio M. Mujal-León is associate professor of government at Georgetown University. He joined the faculty there in 1979 after completing his doctoral studies in the Department of Political Science at the Massachusetts Institute of Technology. During 1984–1986, he was a visiting fellow at the Center of International Studies of Princeton University, working on a project about Soviet–Latin American relations. Professor Mujal-León is the author of numerous articles on Spanish and Portuguese politics as well as on Soviet policy toward Latin America. These have been published in *Orbis, Problems of Communism, Studies in Comparative Communism, The Washington Quarterly,* and *West European Politics.* He has written *Communism and Political Change in Spain* (Indiana University Press, 1983) and *The Cuban University under the Revolution* (University of Miami, 1988). He is also co-editor of *Spain at the Polls* (Duke University Press, 1985) and editor of *Latin American Politics and Society: A Cultural Research Agenda* (a special issue of the journal *World Affairs*) and of *The USSR and Latin America—A Developing Relationship* (Unwin & Hyman, 1989). He is currently working on *Looking beyond the Pyrenees: Spanish Foreign Policy since Franco* (forthcoming) and on another book about European Socialism and the Third World.

Acknowledgments

I am grateful to several friends and colleagues who read and commented on earlier drafts of this monograph. Karl Cerny, J. William Friend, Steven Kramer, Manfred Mols, Kendall Myers, Ann-Sofie Nilsson, and Avner Yaniv gave generously of their time and helped in many ways to improve the manuscript. What errors of fact or interpretation remain are, of course, my responsibility.

Thanks are also due to the Smith Richardson Foundation, which provided me with research support during preparation of this monograph, as well as to the Graduate School at Georgetown University, which also helped with a summer research and travel grant. A note of appreciation is also in order to Howard Wiarda who first encouraged me to think about this subject when he asked me to prepare a chapter for *Rift and Revolution* (American Enterprise Institute, 1984). I also thank a number of research assistants — Alain Belanger, Phyllis Berry, Alan Dillingham, Hernán Gutiérrez, and Johnny Lund — who, over the course of the past three years, have helped me with the research on this monograph.

Summary

The crisis in Central America has afforded numerous transnational, regional, and extracontinental actors the opportunity to become involved in an area traditionally considered a reserve and special zone of influence for the United States. One notable example of this phenomenon has been the engagement fo European Socialist and Social Democratic parties in the region. Their active involvement in Central American issues (and the oppositin many of their leaders have expressed toward U.S. policy in the region) has represented a significant departure for parties that have been broadly supportive of U.S. foreign policy initiatives and objectives since the late 1940s.

This monograph analyzes the Central American policies and perspectives fo the three European Socialist and Social Democratic parties – the Spanish PSOE, the French PS, and the West German SPD – which have been most active in the region. Chapter 1 explores the sources of European Socialist interest in Central America, placing this concern in a historical context that takes into account developments both in Western Europe and in the international Social Democratic movement over the past two decades. Chapters 2 through 4 focus on the parties individually, providing case studies of the initiatives undertaken by the

PSOE, PS, and SPD with respect to Central America. Each of these chapters places the Central American issue in the context of national foreign policy, assessing its relative importance and identifying those factions and personalities within each party that have shaped policy toward that region. The concluding chapter discusses the broader impact and significance of European Socialist engagement in Central America.

Introduction

The crisis in Central America has afforded numerous transnational, regional, and extracontinental actors the opportunity to become involved in an area historically considered a reserve and special zone of influence for the United States. One notable example of this phenomenon has been the engagement of European Socialist and Social Democratic parties in the region. Their active involvement in Central American issues (and the opposition many of their leaders have expressed toward U.S. policy in the region) has represented a significant departure for parties that have been broadly supportive of U.S. foreign policy initiatives and objectives since the late 1940s.

Important though European Socialist engagement on Central American issues (especially visible after the triumph of the Sandinista revolution in July 1979) has been, it has also reflected a much broader trend, visible during the course of the past 15 years, which has put these parties at odds with U.S. policy on many issues, ranging from disarmament and nuclear missile deployments to issues that focus on how to deal with revolutionary change in the Third World.

This monograph analyzes the Central American policies and perspectives of the three European Socialist and

Social Democratic parties – the Spanish Partido Socialista Obrero Español (PSOE), the French Socialist Party (PS), and the West German Social Democratic Party (SPD) – which have been most active in the region. Chapter 1 explores the sources of European Socialist interest in Central America, seeking to place this concern in a historical context that considers developments both in Western Europe and in the international Social Democratic movement during the past two decades. Chapters 2 through 4 focus on individual parties – providing case studies of the initiatives undertaken by the Spanish PSOE, the French PS, and the West German SPD – with respect to Central America. Each of these chapters places the Central American issue in the context of national foreign policy, assessing its relative importance and identifying those factions and personalities within each party that have shaped policy toward that region. The conclusion assesses the impact and significance of European Socialist engagement in Central America.

1

European Socialism and Its International Agenda: The Case of Central America

Why are Europeans and, in particular, European Socialist and Social Democratic parties and leaders so keenly interested in Central American developments, and why have they been willing (indeed, sometimes eager) to challenge U.S. policy in many regions?[1] To answer these questions one must consider several factors: first, the traditions and experiences that have formed the European Social Democratic movement in the twentieth century; second, the domestic and foreign policy adjustments these parties made in the aftermath of World War II to increase their chances for coming to power alone or in coalition governments; third, the impact of the "successor" generation of Socialist activists on their parties' domestic and foreign policy positions; and fourth, how the changes in the self-perception and role of the United States, Latin America, and Western Europe have contributed to European Social Democracy's engagement in Latin (and Central) America.

During the 1980s, European Social Democracy is attempting to reestablish an international influence lost earlier in this century, in the wake of World War I (1914–1918) and the Bolshevik Revolution (1917). Those two events—along with the subsequent economic, political, and moral devastation of Europe during World War II—rendered

Social Democracy a subsidiary actor on the world scene. This was not an easy fate for a movement whose very definition gave it a global perspective and whose ideology had convinced it, in the years prior to World War I, of the inevitability of victory. Led by its flagship, the German SPD, whose organization and theoreticians were points of reference for the entire movement, European Social Democracy was confident of its future hegemony on the European continent and, by implication, the rest of the world. Perusal of the documents issued by individual parties as well as the Second International (of which these parties formed part) confirms both a sense of optimism and the conviction of these parties that they not only understood the laws of history (they were for the most part animated by Marxism, after all) but, more important, that they could claim to speak for the working class and oppressed throughout the world.[2]

The Crisis of Social Democracy

The initial Social Democratic dream – in its European and international dimensions – was shattered by World War I and the Bolshevik Revolution. The former was the first part of a two-act tragedy, subsequently consummated with World War II, that devastated Europe and contributed to its division and subordination after 1945. The Bolshevik Revolution rent the Social Democratic movement apart, and the sectarian tactics of the Bolshevik Party and its adherents (organized after 1919 in the Communist International) weakened the Left, particularly the Socialist and Social Democratic parties.[3]

Under fire from Communists and fascists, and generally distrusted by middle-class parties (not to mention authoritarian sectors in the military, churches, and bureaucracies of individual countries), Social Democracy was generally in retreat throughout Europe during the late 1920s and 1930s. An exception was Sweden where in 1932 the

Social Democratic Worker Party (SAP) began nearly five decades of uninterrupted governmental participation, but this success, as with the Popular Front victories in France and Spain, only underscored the movement's more general vulnerability.

The post-World War II situation was more favorable for European Social Democracy insofar as fascism now lay vanquished and parliamentary democracy had been reestablished. Collaboration between Communists, Socialists, and Catholics in the wartime Resistance movements in France and Italy seemed to open new perspectives for the Left in southern Europe. In the north, Social Democratic parties (especially the German SPD) anticipated a situation where, with the weakening of traditional conservative forces, they could not only reestablish but expand their traditional working-class base. These hopes, however, proved largely unfounded. Events soon demonstrated that the Communist parties of France and Italy had not shed their "Stalinist" identity and remained instruments of Soviet state foreign policy. The imposition of Soviet control over Eastern Europe and the forcible absorption of the Social Democratic parties into Communist organizations, as in East Germany, or into otherwise powerless broad-front organizations, delivered an unmistakable message about the dangers of collaborating with Communists and helped strengthen the hand of conservative, democratic parties throughout Western Europe.[4] For the SPD, in particular, the division of Germany and the onset of the Cold War meant more than the loss of an electoral stronghold in Prussia; it provided a clear boost to West German Chancellor Konrad Adenauer's Christian Democratic Union (CDU).

Accommodation and Adjustment

The stabilization of the domestic situation in Western Europe and the onset of the Cold War impelled the Socialist and Social Democratic parties toward a further adjustment in their domestic and foreign policy perspectives. Reformism became the order of the day, which, in effect, meant making peace with the Keynesian capitalist model, accepting a mixed economy, and eschewing any effort to pursue a radical transformation of social structures. In exchange for such concessions, these parties could help build the welfare state and in some instances take credit for laying its foundations. Here the northern European Social Democratic parties – such as the Swedish SAP and the British Labour Party, and, to a lesser extent, the SPD – took the lead. For its part, the SPD provided the most prominent political symbol of this adjustment, abandoning its self-definition as Marxist, emphasizing the humanist dimension of its ideology, and dropping its commitment to nationalization at the 1959 Bad Godesberg Congress.[5]

By contrast, the southern European Socialist parties found it more difficult to abandon their tradition of radical rhetoric. For the PSOE, the rigors of clandestine opposition to the Franco regime kept the party's ideology anchored in the tumult of the 1930s. The French and Italian Socialist parties (the PS and PSI), for their part, had been in national governments in the postwar period (the PS under the Fourth Republic; the PSI in the 1940s and then again on and off after 1963), but theirs were countries with strong revolutionary traditions and sharply ideological politics. Not until the 1970s, when democracy came to the Iberian peninsula and the challenge posed by the Communists had begun to recede throughout southern Europe (either because the Eurocommunist message had become indistinguishable from the democratic socialist one at the programmatic level, or because the traditional Communist support base had become visibly weaker, or both), did these parties shift the tone of their ideological pronouncements and openly embrace reformism.

Another aspect of Social Democracy's adjustment was evident in the realm of foreign policy, where those parties in countries that signed the North Atlantic Treaty (1949) soon accepted and eventually gave strong support to participation in the Atlantic Alliance. Moderation in domestic policy and alignment with the United States, as well as adherence to the principles of the alliance, were important steps that helped to legitimize the European Socialist and Social Democratic parties after World War II and allowed them to compete for national power. In this respect, the case of the SPD is again, if not typical, at least instructive. Having been initially adamant about supporting the reunification of the two Germanies and opposing rearmament (in either a European or Atlantic version), the SPD changed its views during the 1950s. By the time of the Bad Godesberg Congress in 1959, the Social Democrats had become supporters of European integration and had developed a more positive approach toward national defense issues as well as NATO.[6]

Generally weaker in southern Europe than in the northern countries, the European Socialist and Social Democratic family expanded its political and social base during the 1950s and 1960s; many parties became viable contenders for national power, and others assumed at least a share of governmental responsibility. Their political integration had a profound effect on national politics and on the parties themselves. It also spawned the idea that European politics was becoming less ideological, and left-wing parties (to achieve success) were becoming catchall organizations, abandoning whatever pretensions they might have had for effecting systemic or structural change.[7]

Predictions are hazardous — particularly concerning political systems. The "end of ideology" theorists had extrapolated a model for the future based on a snapshot — a description of what was. Their focus on postindustrial society correctly assumed important social and economic dynamics were taking place in Western Europe. What was more, their intuition that new issues were emerging around which political competition would be organized in coming decades was prescient. They were wrong, however, about the implications that they drew from the behavior of Social Democracy (especially northern European) after 1945. True, many of the northern Social Democratic parties had moderated their economic and social programs, adapting and contributing to as well as benefiting from the construction of the welfare state edifice. But the expansion that had allowed for the relatively painless creation of the welfare state began to slow during the late 1960s, and the economic downturn accelerated during the 1970s. Instead of presiding over expansion and increased opportunities for redistribution, Social Democracy had to cope with stagflation and budget cutbacks (the case of the SPD from 1974 to 1982 is again instructive, but so is the example of the SAP and the British Labour Party).

New Perspectives and a Successor Generation

The crisis of the welfare state had profound consequences for European Social Democracy. It had gained support and had legitimized its moderate policies (both to the electorates and the party memberships) largely through economic successes. With national economies in a slump, this was no longer possible. But the problem went deeper than merely adjusting an electoral message. Socialist and Social Democratic party leaderships now confronted a younger generation of politically active people for whom the economic accomplishments of the preceding decades were, if not unimportant, at least taken for granted. Their concerns were not with economic production, but rather with the quality of life and the impact of the industrial system on the environment and society.[8] Underlying these concerns was an anticapitalist bias with intellectual roots not only in a socialist but also in a preindustrial, romantic tradition. This combination of ideas both fueled and fed on student protests throughout Western Europe in the late 1960s and early 1970s.

This "successor" generation also developed certain reflexes or intuitions about foreign policy that were significant for the Socialist and Social Democratic movement in Western Europe. It did not have a vivid memory of the postwar period and of the role the United States played in the reconstruction and defense of Western Europe.[9] To many of these activists, the United States and the Soviet Union were essentially equivalent superpowers, both of whom wished to keep Europe divided and subordinate. Similarly, with their energies galvanized through opposition to the U.S. role in the Vietnam War, many had romantic notions about the Third World, identifying with revolutionary movements there and their struggle against imperialism.

The incorporation of this younger generation of activists affected Socialist and Social Democratic parties throughout Western Europe. Obviously, the impact varied from country to country – it depended on the way established party leaders handled the situation and on the state of national politics. What cannot be denied is that the more utopian and idealistic notions of this younger generation struck a resonant chord throughout the movement.

Why was this so? Briefly, because after 1914, European Social Democracy had suffered from (and in some ways engaged in) a collective amnesia that had led it to suppress one of those qualities that distinguishes socialism, provides it with strength, and lends it a utopian dimension: the capacity to dream, to generate idealism and illusion. Although cynics might scoff, this capacity is at the core of socialism, be it inspired by Marxism or some other doctrine. After 1914, the Socialist and Social Democratic movement in Western Europe had to surrender many of its illusions and dreams, such as the idea that pacifist conviction and international solidarity could prevent war and that the working class could and would act as a united domestic and international force. Later, the struggle for survival against fascism and communism, although allowing for the definition and refinement of Social Democracy's commitment to democratic values and parliamentary democracy (already presaged in Eduard Bernstein's 1899 revisionist classic, *Evolutionary Socialism*, and confirmed in Karl Kautsky's post-World War I text, *The Dictatorship of the Proletariat*, which sharply criticized the Russian Revolution), caused it to downplay the utopian component of its ideology.

The post-World War II context reinforced the trend toward adjustment and accommodation, but not even in the
most reformist party was the utopian vision – the thirst for
change and illusion – altogether lost. Socialists and Social
Democrats might have accommodated to the postwar
world, but they still retained their sense of purpose and
importance. Pacifism and neutralism, for example, themes
at the heart of the Second International's congresses in the
first two decades of this century, remained important traditions, as did the antimilitarist strain of the movement. Here
again one can cite the debates in the SPD in the late 1950s
and early 1960s on rearmament, but these traditions were
also present in other parties.

Submerged but never entirely abandoned, these traditions sprang back to life in the late 1960s and 1970s, especially in the northern European countries. They found expression in the Federal Republic of Germany – where as
articulated by the left wing of the SPD and its youth wing,
the Jungsozialisten (JUSOS), and later by the Greens, it
became, at least partially, an expression of German nationalism. In Sweden, Prime Minister Olof Palme used these
ideas in trying to turn his country into a "moral superpower."[10] The incorporation of the "new politics" groups played a
major role in reawakening these traditions and issues
among Socialist and Social Democratic parties.

The Communist Question Revisited

The question of how Democratic Socialists should relate to
revolutionary Marxists assumed importance once again
during the late 1960s and the 1970s. In southern Europe,
for example, the debate centered on whether the Socialists
should join in broad political or electoral fronts with Communist parties. Taking the lead on this issue was the
French Socialist Party. Under the leadership of François
Mitterrand after the July 1971 Epinay Congress, it sub-

scribed to a *Programme Commun* with the Communists in 1972, thereafter jointly contesting several parliamentary elections.[11] French Socialist collaboration with the Communists and their criticisms of the SPD-led West German government's economic policies for serving interests other than those of the working class led to embarrassing public disputes between the two parties, eventually directly involving President François Mitterrand and Chancellor Helmut Schmidt.[12]

Developments in the late 1970s rendered SPD-PS conflicts on these issues moot. The West German Social Democrats pursued their own contacts with both the ruling Communist parties in Eastern Europe and the Italian Communist Party (PCI). The Socialist-Communist alliance disintegrated, even before Mitterrand had won election to the presidency in May 1981. By then, too, the balance had inclined against collaboration with the Communists throughout southern Europe. In France, the entente had dissolved acrimoniously. In Italy, the PSI had cast a wary eye at its vastly stronger (on the order of three to one in voters' preferences in 1976) Communist rival's proposals for a "historic compromise" with the other giant of Italian politics, the Christian Democrats. In Spain, the memories of Communist conduct during the Spanish Civil War (1936–1939) remained vivid and, despite pressures from some activists, party leader Felipe González concluded that his PSOE had more to lose than to gain from joint ventures with his country's small Communist Party. It was in Portugal, however, where the most bitter experience occurred after the April 1974 revolution had overthrown the corporatist-fascist *Estado Novo*. There, the Communist Party, in alliance with radical military officers in the Armed Forces Movement, tried to implant a new dictatorship. The Portuguese Socialist Party (PSP) and its leader, Mário Soares, played a key role in thwarting those efforts, emerging from the experience as a stalwart opponent of collaboration with Communists.

Direct experience with Communists was an inoculant for

the reinvigorated southern European Socialists of the 1970s and 1980s. The Northern European parties were more fortunate in this respect: at least they did not have to deal with the challenge posed by strong Communist parties. Even these parties, however, could not altogether ignore the Communist issue. The SAP relied on Communist parliamentary support to govern in the early 1970s, and a decade later in the Federal Republic of Germany, there developed a strong debate within the SPD as well as between the SPD and its youth branch (JUSOS) over the desirability and advisability of joint actions with the German Communist Party (DKP) on disarmament and other questions. Here the new SPD generation tended to favor (or at least to tolerate) such initiatives.

A second aspect of the Communist question related to Social Democracy's relations with the myriad ultra-Left and "direct action" groups that had proliferated in the late 1960s and early 1970s. The more benign among them, although espousing Trotskyite or Maoist ideas, never moved toward terrorism. Others, ranging from the Red Brigades to the Baader-Meinhof gang, combined Marxism, radical Christian ideas, and a healthy dose of nihilism as they moved toward violence. The mainstream of European Socialist and Social Democratic parties roundly condemned such activities, but there were intellectuals (usually on the left-wing fringe of these movements or active in the youth wings) who explained or at least rationalized the emergence of these terrorist groups as an outgrowth of capitalist society.

The third and final aspect of the Communist question for European Social Democracy had an international rather than domestic dimension. Centered on the Third World, it focused on the desirability (or inevitability) of dictatorships and violent change in various regions of the world. For the most part, the dilemmas—reform or revolution, democracy or dictatorship—had been resolved in Western Europe after World War II. Indeed, the Eurocommunist phenomenon represented a belated recognition of this very reality by several European Communist parties.

But if democracy had become a consolidated reality in Western Europe, democratic reform movements in the Third World shone by their absence. Violence, instability, and revolution were the order of the day there. Attention focused on national liberation movements that fought not only for their countries' political and economic independence but against what presumably were corrupt and unrepresentative oligarchies.

The Third World as an Arena of Engagement

The incorporation of younger left-wing activists into the European Socialist and Social Democratic parties coincided with the reemergence of the Third World as an arena of policy concern. In their political socialization, the Vietnam War had played a crucial role. It glorified revolutionary violence and struggle. It also galvanized the political energies of an entire generation, profoundly changing European perceptions of the United States. No longer was the United States the country primarily responsible for the defeat of fascism and the consolidation of democracy in Western Europe. It had become the established, dominant, and dominating power, seeking in a manner not unlike the Soviet Union's to impose its will on smaller countries. Support for Third World countries and national liberation movements was the inescapable choice for a movement that considered itself an advocate of the underdog, supportive of programs designed to enhance both domestic "social solidarity" and the international redistribution of wealth.

With these changes in attitude came a shift in focus toward the Third World and the idealization of revolutionary movements there. True, European Socialist and Social Democratic parties had a long anticolonial and anti-imperialist heritage, but this tradition had lain dormant in more recent years. Some parties, especially those whose countries had little or no colonial tradition, focused their energies almost exclusively on domestic reconstruction and development. Others (and the French Socialists' ordeal with respect to Vietnam and Algeria in the 1940s and 1950s comes to mind) had a more painful experience. The French Socialists' experience arose from their participation in the government during the decolonization process itself.[13]

The reawakened interest in the former colonial areas resulted in intensified demands for a more equitable distribution of economic wealth between the developed North and the underdeveloped South and for active political solidarity with national liberation movements.[14] Generally speaking, European Socialists came to share certain attitudes about the Third World and the United States. They believed that

• narrowing the gap between the rich and poor nations had become "the social question of the [20th] century";[15]
• the United States did not understand (or, in its more extreme form, could not and would not understand) what was happening in the Third World;
• most conflicts in the Third World were locally generated and had indigenous social and economic causes;
• the United States was eager to bring the East-West conflict into Third World arenas in part because it was eager to reassert its faltering hegemony over the western alliance; and
• East-West confrontations in the Third World were also dangerous because they threatened to torpedo vital negotiations over arms control and disarmament, weakening Western Europe and lessening its room to maneuver in the process.

Such themes were common to all members of the Democratic Socialist family in Western Europe, but they probably found their strongest echo among the northern European Social Democratic parties. For these parties, the economic crisis of the 1970s had created a dilemma. They could either adjust their sights downward and accept the "crisis" of the welfare state or advance toward a more "socialist" agenda, domestically and internationally. Thus, during the 1970s, just as the southern European Socialist parties were coming closer to power, abandoning radical Marxist rhetoric, and recognizing the length of the journey that lay ahead as they tried to modernize their countries, the northern Social Democrats were intensifying their ideological commitments, at least partially in response to frustration over the potential exhaustion of the welfare state model. In this respect, the numerical and sociological insignificance of Communist parties and extreme Left movements in northern Europe also had the paradoxical effect of rendering Social Democratic parties more vulnerable to the importing of radical ideas directly into their organizations. At the same time, as deeply as these ideas may have been held by many in the SAP and the SPD, concern for and solidarity with the Third World were also vehicles to express their frustration with a stagnated domestic agenda and to direct the energies of their more radical (or idealistic) party members outward.

If the "crisis" of the welfare state encouraged northern European Social Democratic parties to look toward the Third World, several other circumstances also contributed to their Third World activism. One was the strong internationalist tradition of these parties. Because they were wealthier and better organized than their southern counterparts, receiving substantial state subsidies for themselves and the foundations to which they were linked, the SPD and SAP (again mentioning only the most prominent examples) also had greater financial and political resources at their disposal for international activity. The northern European moralistic traditions were also relevant. Finally, because they were more distant geographically, historically, and even culturally, the northern parties had fewer reasons to adopt ambiguous positions concerning specific Third World issues.

Solidarity with Revolutionary Movements

The prominent German Social Democrat Kurt Schumacher once referred to Communists and Social Democrats as brothers, "like Cain and Abel." A French phrase likewise refers to Socialists and Communists as *frères-ennemis*. These formulations aptly captured the essence of post-1917 relations, but from them can also be inferred a continuing sense of engagement and concern with revolutionary Marxists. Communists have been and are a point of reference for Social Democracy, often negative but always there.

As the European Social Democrats shifted their attention to the Third World, several strains in Social Democratic thought, submerged since the 1920s, reappeared. One was the notion that although revolutionary regimes were abhorrent, their excesses and existence were more or less justified, considering the nature of the autocratic governments that preceded them. The British Fabian G. D. H. Cole, for example, maintained that the "cost of immediate sufferings, of terrible inhumanities to alleged enemies of the Revolution, and of the growth of a stifling political structure of espionage and police control" was "largely unavoidable," and he extolled the Russian Revolution as "a great and glorious achievement," an "immense and liberating force."[16] Similar language may be found in the Resolutions and Manifestos of the Labour and Socialist International (LSI) in the late 1920s and early 1930s. Thus in 1928 the LSI's Manifesto noted how "the parties united within (it) are now ready to defend the Soviet Republic against any hostility on the part of capitalist governments and to defend it against any counter-revolution or aggression, and also to demand from all states the maintenance of peaceful and normal relations with it."[17] Even a Menshevik-sponsored resolution at the 1923 LSI Congress criticized "attempts by the imperialist powers to intervene in the internal affairs of Russia or to instigate a new civil war in Russia," even as it urged the Congress to express "its warmest sympathies with all

SOCIALIST victims of the Bolshevik reign of terror in Russia and Georgia [emphasis added]."[18]

The shift in focus toward the Third World revived the vocabulary of anti-imperialism among European Socialists and Social Democrats. Condemnations of imperialism had regularly found their way into Second International documents prior to World War I, and they remained even as these parties assumed governmental responsibilities. Anti-imperialist denunciations had coexisted alongside a belief that decolonization was not urgent, would come in time, and that the relationship with Europe had beneficial effects for the colonies. The tutelary sense was lost neither easily nor quickly. Witness the French Socialist attitude toward Algeria in the 1950s and toward the Francophone community in Africa during the early 1980s, or even the Dutch Socialist position with respect to their Caribbean possessions in the 1970s. Nevertheless, once most European countries had lost or given up their major colonies, it became easier for European Socialist and Social Democratic parties to express their anti-imperialist convictions. Most European countries had lost or given up their major colonies by the early 1960s. Moreover, it was now the United States that, having become deeply engaged in the Third World, could be targeted as the imperial hegemony.

The European Socialists Rediscover America

By the 1970s, European Democratic Socialism had clearly begun to stir, with many of its members rediscovering their roots as parties that desired to transform domestic and international society. During this process, the movement shifted its attention toward the Third World, actively seeking partners and interlocutors there. This shift in Democratic Socialist perspectives coincided with changes in both the European and international environments, some of which have already been alluded to or mentioned. In Western Europe, there was a resurgence of nationalist sentiment that had been largely submerged since the onset of the Cold War. Articulated only partly in traditional nation-state terms, the phenomenon was only incidentally anti-American. It reflected instead a pan-European sensibility at whose fountainhead lay the desire to reassert the Continent's identity, and this entailed an effort both to mark Europe's distance from the United States and to emphasize the distinctiveness of its problems and vulnerabilities. Such political assertiveness transcended ideology, becoming a shared value among Christian Democrats, Gaullists, Liberals, Social Democrats, and even some Communists, especially in Italy.

Such assertiveness, which was accompanied by the emergence of the European Community (EC) and individual Western European countries as major forces in the international economy, led to intensified European involvement in international politics. As mentioned earlier, the Vietnam War had alienated important sectors of West European public and elite opinion, raised doubts in others about U.S. judgment and leadership. Pursuit of détente had meanwhile also increased fissiparous tendencies within the Atlantic Alliance. At first, some Europeans feared that détente would lead to superpower condominium. Following the Soviet invasion of Afghanistan (1979) and the declaration of martial law in Poland (1981), many thought that the growing confrontation between the United States and the Soviet Union would sharply narrow Europe's room for maneuverability vis-à-vis the two superpowers. The response was a deepened sense of pan-European nationalism and increasing engagement in Third World issues. Intensified involvement in the Middle East and southern Africa, disputes over "out-of-area" responsibilities (not to mention the debates over arms control and disarmament issues that have convulsed the Atlantic Alliance since the late 1970s) attested to this phenomenon.

Latin America was among the Third World areas to which Western Europe increasingly turned its reinvigorated attention in the 1970s.[19] Renewed European interest in the region (and the positive response countries and institutions there gave to these overtures) signaled an end to the historical parenthesis that had begun with the consolidation of U.S. influence over both Latin America and Western Europe earlier in this century.[20]

Western Europe approached Latin America from several perspectives.[21] There was, for example, an economic rationale behind pursuit of the Latin American connection. Over the preceding two decades, Western Europe had become an economic superpower, its growth fueled by a nearly constant expansion in exports. By the early 1970s, no less than 22 percent of the EC's gross domestic product (GDP) was trade-related. The European search for markets intensified after the 1973 oil price hikes and the subsequent fluctuation in the prices of raw materials and energy products. Under these circumstances, exports became all the more crucial in sustaining Europe's growth and its quest for a new international role.[22] And in this context, Latin America—a continent of 350 million people, with a combined GDP of approximately $250 billion and one of the most economically advanced regions in the Third World—became an important target.[23]

More important than economic considerations, however, were the political reasons for Western Europe's engagement with Latin America. There was, in the first place, the sense that the region was the most "European" area in the Third World, with institutions, cultural values, and political problems similar to those that confronted southern European countries well into the twentieth century. This raised expectations about greater possibilities for dialogue and understanding. Enhancing such prospects was the resurgence of Latin American nationalism and the emergence of middle, subregional powers such as Argentina, Brazil, Mexico, and Venezuela in the early 1970s—circumstances that testified both to the weakening of the old inter-American system and to the growing multipolarity of the international one. These countries (and their leaders) were eager to develop such alternative economic and political relationships, all the more because Western European countries had no capacity for imperial action. Under these circumstances, the European connection could be used, not only to impart international legitimacy (almost an imprimatur) but as an effective counterbalance to the United States.

For the Europeans, in turn, the absence of any direct security or strategic interests or exposure in the region made engagement a virtually risk-free proposition. Moreover, given the almost inevitably problematic relations Latin America would have with the United States, Western Europe could hardly be other than a desirable partner. The existence of well-organized parties in Latin America (there were strong Christian Democratic organizations in Venezuela and Chile, Social Democratic ones in Venezuela and Costa Rica, and the "populist-nationalist" Acción Popular Revolucionaria Americana or APRA in Peru and the Partido Revolucionario Institucional or PRI in Mexico) provided an additional incentive to those European parties seeking partners or interlocutors.

Of those European political groups that looked toward Latin America in the 1970s, none did so with greater enthusiasm and sense of opportunity than the Democratic Socialist family. There were historic links between some Latin American parties and the international movement. For the Argentinian and Uruguayan Socialist parties these ties dated to the 1920s; the British Labour Party was quite active in the Caribbean during the 1940s and 1950s; the Socialist International (SI) created a Latin American Secretariat in 1955; and Venezuela's Democratic Action (AD) and Costa Rica's National Liberation Party (PLN) developed contacts with the Socialist International during the 1950s and 1960s.[24] But these contacts had developed unevenly and without great intensity.

The situation began to change in the early 1970s. One important event in this regard was Salvador Allende's election to the Chilean presidency at the head of the Popular

Unity coalition in late 1970. The SI (whose Chilean member was the Radical Party, not Allende's Socialist Party) welcomed his election. Wary about his collaboration with the Communists and the radical tendencies of Allende's own party, the SI nevertheless emphasized its support for his efforts to lead Chile on a peaceful transition to socialism. As a show of solidarity, the SI's highest policy-making body (the Bureau) met in Santiago in February 1973, the first time ever in Latin America. Much like the Spanish Civil War nearly four decades earlier, the September 1973 military coup that overthrew Allende galvanized international (and European) attention and solidarity. Chile became a rallying point for the European Socialist movement. An SI delegation headed by French Socialist Antoine Blanca traveled to Chile barely a month after the coup; SPD leader Hans-Jürgen Wischnewski pointedly visited political prisoners held on Chile's Dawson Island; SI Vice President Sicco Mansholt (Holland) headed another SI delegation to Santiago in March 1975 and thereafter recommended an international economic boycott against Chile; and the SAP began a program of refugee support that led to the emigration of nearly 15,000 Chileans to that country.[25]

The Chilean tragedy encouraged European socialism toward deeper and more comprehensive engagement in Latin America. It also provided additional impetus to the efforts of several Social Democratic leaders (most prominently West German Chancellor Willy Brandt, but he did so in active collaboration with Austrian Chancellor Bruno Kreisky and Olof Palme) who tried to articulate a "Third Way" strategy for both Western Europe and its Social Democratic movement. This was the theme of their volume of correspondence entitled *Briefe und Gespräche* (1975).[26] The idea was timely and struck a sensitive and sympathetic chord among many Social Democrats. For one thing, the proposals contained in the correspondence offered an "offensive" vision to the movement and, more particularly, to their respective parties.[27] Social Democracy was not just about accommodation and adjustment. It was interested in modifying social and economic structure as well as Western Europe's relations with the United States and the Third World. Social Democracy also disposed of a vehicle (the Socialist International) through which to pursue discussions with Third World parties and movements. As Brandt put it:

> Let us take the example of Central America. There are many countries there with parties which are close to what we call democratic socialism. But they do not enter into a framework as rigid as that of the International upon which weighs so strongly the influence of its tradition. Consequently, we must find a way to allow our parties and a group of parties from those countries to arrive at an exchange of views.[28]

The European Socialist drive for engagement in Latin America gained further momentum from the active and successful role its member parties played in the Spanish and Portuguese transitions to democracy and in the rise of potent Socialist parties in those countries during the mid-1970s. Mário Soares and Felipe González were relatively unknown figures and their parties weak organizations in the early 1970s when they began to receive systematic organizational and political support from their European co-religionists, in particular from the SPD. The PSP held its constituent congress in September 1973 at a Friedrich Ebert Stiftung meetinghouse outside of Bonn. The SPD also played a major, if not decisive, role in having the SI recognize the PSOE (or, more precisely, the "renovator" faction headed by Felipe González) as its official Spanish member in 1974. Following the April 1974 military coup in Portugal, the SPD was again instrumental in providing assistance to these parties, relying on the Ebert Stiftung and its trade union affiliate (the Deutscher Gewerkschaftsbund or DGB) to provide resources for developing cadres and infrastructure. This support, which probably exceeded $10 million in the Portuguese case and $20 million in the Spanish in the mid and late 1970s,[29] enabled these parties to withstand challenges from otherwise better-organized Communist organizations.

European Socialism's Iberian experience set the scene for its Central American *mise-en-scène* (staging) in the late 1970s. From it, the movement emerged with a great boost to its self-confidence. Unlike the United States, which had been unable to extricate itself from an entangling alliance with both authoritarian regimes, Western Europe (particularly the Social Democratic parties that were still ascendant in the north) had played an unassailably positive role. Social Democracy's engagement had helped to ensure not only democracy's victory in Iberia but also the consolidation of strong Socialist parties. The verdict was almost too good to be true, and in the late 1970s, the movement was ready to export the model to warmer climes.

The Socialists and Central America

Central America had become a major Third World crisis spot by the late 1970s. The July 1979 Sandinista victory in Nicaragua appeared to presage revolutionary changes throughout the region. Economic turmoil and political instability characterized nearly all the countries there. The one exception, Costa Rica, an island of democracy with no standing army, was in danger of becoming engulfed in its neighbors' quarrels. Further compounding the situation, the region had become an arena of superpower competition. Of vital strategic importance to the United States, Central America had nevertheless been ignored by successive U.S. administrations, most of whom cared little about encouraging economic development in the region as long as stability was maintained.

Since the early 1960s, however, Fidel Castro had provided financial and organizational support to various insurgent movements in the region. One of these, the Frente Sandinista de Liberación Nacional or FSLN, had reached power in 1979. Another, the Farabundo Martí National Liberation Front (FMLN) sought to duplicate this feat by launching a "final offensive" in the last days of the Carter administration. When Ronald Reagan assumed the presidency of the United States in January 1981, he confronted not only a deepening crisis in the Central American region but also a rising chorus of criticism from European Social Democracy.

The European Socialist and Social Democratic parties shared certain perspectives about the crisis in Central America.

- For them, the principal cause of the crisis in the region lay in the inequitable distribution of wealth. Underdeveloped and dependent economic structures formed the basis for political and social control wielded by narrow domestic oligarchies.
- These oligarchies had been historically unwilling to allow the expansion of popular participation, and they drew on the Communist danger as a vehicle for reinforcing U.S. commitment to their survival.
- The United States (particularly the Reagan administration) had come late to the side of democracy in the region, and its efforts with respect to Nicaragua were ill-considered and immoral.
- Even if the Nicaraguan FSLN had close relations with Cuba and the Soviet Union and even if the FSLN had moved to consolidate a leftist authoritarian regime in the country, the United States had no right to intervene in Nicaragua's domestic affairs.
- Such intervention only reinforced the more hard-line elements of the FSLN leadership.
- Neither Cuba nor the Soviet Union wished to see a radicalization of the Nicaraguan revolution or the extension of armed conflict throughout the region. It was, therefore, possible that a negotiated settlement (attained through the auspices of the Contadora Group) might be possible.
- Such a settlement would allow the FSLN a relatively free hand within Nicaragua (with the possibility, in the Eu-

ropean Socialist view, of a "Mexican solution"), and in return the FSLN would refrain from intervening in its neighbors' affairs.

These views represent an ideal type of the mindset that major European Socialist and Social Democratic parties and personalities brought to the discussion of Central American issues. To be sure, not all of the parties or individuals concerned held these views with the same intensity, nor did they approach the United States and Latin America in the same way. Various factors conditioned their specific policies and attitudes. It mattered, for example, whether a given party was in the government, whether it ruled alone or in coalition, or whether the party was in the opposition. In the last case, its responsibilities are fewer and criticism becomes a more natural style. Significant, too, were the political culture and predispositions of the country in which the party operated, as well as its degree of ideological and political cohesion. The party's role in the party system and its relations with others on the Left were also relevant. Did a given party face significant competition — among voters, and in the trade unions and universities — from Communist or other extreme Left groups? What was the international agenda of the party in question? How deep were its ties to Central America and which instruments were available for exercising influence in the region? Finally, what was the nature of the party's (and its country's) relationship to the United States, and how did this affect both its outlook and the U.S. response?

2

Spanish Socialism:
The Politics of Cultural Affinity

The PSOE and its First Secretary Felipe González have become prominent figures on the Central American scene in the past decade. Because of its own experience under General Francisco Franco's nearly 40-year dictatorship in Spain and the role it played during the Spanish transition to democracy, the PSOE has assumed a long-standing responsibility for contributing to the democratization of those Latin and Central American countries currently, or until recently, ruled by authoritarian regimes. The Socialists partake of a historic Spanish desire, whether expressed in the form of the Francoist neocolonialist concept of *hispanidad* or in its more recent variant of *hispanismo democrático*, to extend Spain's cultural and political influence in the New World.

Spanish Socialist foreign policy has operated in a domestic environment marked by a tradition of isolation and isolationism, growing Europeanization, latent anti-Americanism, and a desire to function as a bridge to the Third World.[1] The PSOE emerged Janus-like from clandestinity in the 1970s — one face emphasizing moderation and modernization, the other promising a radical restructuring of Spain's domestic and foreign policies. This tension between revolution and reform had long been present in the party and indeed had nearly destroyed it during the tumultuous

1930s. Of course, opposition to Franco could be unyielding, and calls for a complete break with the past persisted, as long as there was little realistic chance of change in the regime. As the post-Franco era loomed on the horizon during the 1970s, the contrast sharpened between revolutionary rhetoric and reformist practice. Finally, with the onset of democracy and the parliamentary elections in June 1977, the balance inclined clearly in favor of moderation in domestic policy.

In foreign affairs, however, the PSOE continued to indulge in more radical rhetoric through the 1970s, emphasizing its strong neutralist convictions and sharp criticisms of the United States in numerous programmatic documents. Thus, for example, the PSOE's December 1976 Congress Resolution called for Spanish neutrality, alignment with the underdeveloped South in its struggle with the advanced industrial countries of the North, and closer ties with "Mediterranean Socialist" forces such as the Syrian and Iraqi Ba'th parties. The same resolution "condemned U.S. imperialist intervention in Latin America" and identified the party with an international working class that found itself under "the permanent aggression of International Capitalism" and its "imperialist expression" (presumably a reference to the United States).[2]

The 1976 Congress also referred to Latin America: It condemned the "imperialist intervention of the United States," proclaimed a future "democratic Spain's solidarity with all those peoples who continue to struggle to free themselves from oppression by local tyrannies at the service of imperialist interests," and promised them concrete measures of "moral and, when possible, material support."[3] During this period, the Socialists retained the view that conflict with the United States – particularly about its policies in Latin America – was inevitable and, indeed, necessary. Even González, who generally avoided confrontation and strident rhetoric, pointedly referred to Puerto Rico as a U.S. colony during a speech at the 1978 Socialist International Congress.[4] Other Socialists put things in even sharper perspective. For example, Miguel Angel Martínez, who became the party's spokesman in the Congress of Deputies after the 1982 election victory, called on Spain "to support the anti-imperialist struggle of Latin American peoples against the U.S.," and concluded that "it [was] inevitable [for Spain] to confront the United States as [it] developed a Latin American policy."[5]

Although declaratory radicalism (particularly about Central America) remained in vogue in the PSOE through the late 1970s, there was nevertheless a perceptible shift toward a less confrontational posture in the years immediately before the Socialists won the October 1982 elections. Various factors contributed to this shift. One was the consolidation of Felipe González's control over the PSOE. First elected party secretary in 1974, González had declined re-election at the 28th PSOE Congress in May 1979 after the delegates had rejected his recommendation that the party drop Marxism from its programmatic self-definition. Subsequently, González had won a convincing personal victory at the Extraordinary 29th Congress four months later, when the assembled delegates concurred with his original idea. The elimination of Marxism was an important symbol for the PSOE. It implied that the party was ready to jettison radical demands (and the possibility of alliance with the Communist Party) and to adopt a definitively reformist platform whose principal objective was the modernization of Spanish society.

A man of pragmatic and moderate intuitions, González learned a great deal about foreign policy during the first years of Spanish democracy. The experience of leading the major Spanish opposition party and his increased exposure to the international scene contributed to both González's and his party's moderation. Like it or not, the Socialists could not ignore either Ronald Reagan's election victory in November 1980 or the consequent hardening of U.S. policy in Central America. Growing U.S. involvement and the injection of an even greater East-West dimension to the crisis there considerably diminished the role Spain (and other European countries) could hope to play. Closer now to the responsibilities of power, the PSOE leadership and González, in particular, also recognized that, whatever their views on Central America, confrontation with the United States was undesirable. Spain had many more pressing problems (among them, the dilemma over participation in NATO, Gibraltar, still-pending negotiations for entry into the EC, and the ensuring of the defense of Ceuta and Melilla from possible Moroccan attack) on its foreign policy agenda than Central America. Conflict with the United States would only make their resolution more difficult.

A restrained approach also resulted from a change in Spanish Socialist attitudes on East-West issues. During the mid-1970s the PSOE had emphasized its neutralist convictions – it was a posture that struck a positive chord among many Spaniards, especially on the Left. For them, the Soviet threat in Europe or elsewhere was not very real, nor was there a strong sense of shared values with the United States. In the view of the Spanish Left, the United States had done precious little to oust or even to weaken Franco in the immediate postwar years; actually, through the 1953 Base Agreements, it had contributed decisively to the consolidation of the regime. The PSOE shared this sentiment, which encouraged its expressions of neutralism and anti-Americanism. On the other hand, by the late 1970s and early 1980s, partly as a result of the process described earlier and partly because the onset of democracy helped to dissipate the frustration and anger of earlier years, the Socialists began to view an alliance between the Europe of which Spain formed part and the United States as not only necessary but desirable. As González declared in 1984:

> Spain has to make a contribution to the common security of that part of the world to which it belongs – and that is what Spain will do. . . . [I]f [Spain] wishes to be a political, economic, institutional and cultural part of Europe's destiny, then [it] must also make a contribution to that European destiny in terms of security poli-

cy. We are a member of NATO and in addition to that
we have a bilateral military tie to the United States.
That firms up our responsibility for Western security.[6]

Security implied a recognition of threat – in Western
Europe and elsewhere. It also corresponded to a growing
Socialist concern with the expansion of Soviet (and Cuban)
influence in Central America and the Caribbean. Although
often constrained by the presence of an active Socialist left
wing, PSOE leaders increasingly recognized U.S. security
concerns in the region as well as the desirability of minimiz-
ing the Soviet-Cuban role there. Their arguments in support of the Contadora process, for example, emphasized its
roots in "democratic countries which have, at the very least,
as much interest as the United States in braking a possible
Communist advance."[7] González extended the argument
further:

> There are no loose pieces in the Central American puz-
> zle. United States' interests are not just the subjective
> ones of a powerful country that wants to control a spe-
> cific parcel from the point of view of its security; there
> are also objective strategic interests that involve the
> future of the Panama Canal.[8]

Accompanying these changes in Spanish Socialist
perspective was an evident shift in their attitude toward
Fidel Castro and the Cuban Revolution. Ever since his
triumphal entry into Havana in January 1959, Castro had
been lionized in Spain. The Franco regime allowed an otherwise tightly controlled press to extol Castro's virtues; and
then, as if trying to make a point about his regime's commitment to the Iberoamerican community and its independence vis-à-vis the United States, Franco refused to join in
the U.S.-sponsored embargo against Cuba. The younger
generation of Socialist leaders that took control of the
PSOE organization in the early 1970s had been steeped in
the mythology of Castro, the romantic revolutionary, the
man who had given expression to Cuban nationalism (they

either ignored his dictatorial rule or condoned it by blaming the United States) and successfully implemented his regime's policies despite strong U.S. opposition.

By the early 1980s, however, PSOE leaders were no longer as easily smitten by the Cuban Revolution. Leftist intellectuals such as Fernando Claudín – head of the PSOE's Pablo Iglesias Foundation – openly called on the Spanish Left to "shake [itself] of the Cuban syndrome."[9] This intellectual effervescence (admittedly, less intense than what occurred among leftist intellectuals in France during the same period) had the effect of encouraging Socialist leaders to focus a more critical eye on Castro and his revolution and to question the objectives of his revolutionary allies in Central America.

By the October 1982 election (at which time the PSOE won an absolute majority of the seats in the Congress of Deputies), the Socialists had toned down their foreign policy rhetoric. Thereafter, the Felipe González-led PSOE government, reelected with only a slightly diminished majority in June 1986, deepened its pragmatic orientation in the pursuit of international objectives. The best example of this moderation was the Socialist shift on the question of Spain's permanence in NATO. Since the late 1970s, the PSOE had actively opposed such membership and, before taking power, had promised to call a referendum in the wake of which Spain would withdraw from NATO. Once in power, however, the party leadership changed its mind on this score, and by the time the NATO referendum was held in March 1986, the government successfully campaigned for continued, albeit conditional, Spanish membership in the organization.[10]

The Roots of Spanish Socialist Central American Policy

When the Socialists took power, Spain stood ready to assume an active role in Central America. The Socialists shared the more general Spanish interest in the region, but they also brought new and particular concerns to Spain's policy there. One was the belief that, having made a decisive contribution to the transition to democracy in Spain, they could and should strive to make a similar effort on behalf of Latin America. Moreover, of the various parties that emerged with democracy, the Socialists had the strongest links to Latin America, especially with groups and parties in Venezuela and Mexico, where sizable republican contingents had settled after the end of the civil war. Despite these historic links, however, the PSOE developed systematic contacts with Latin American parties and movements relatively late, in the mid-1970s, as it began to function more openly in the twilight of the Franco era. For example, the first official PSOE delegation to visit Latin America only traveled there in 1975. An early problem confronting the party was the weakness of organizational infrastructures through which to sustain and expand its international ties. Personal rather than institutional relationships remained at the core of the PSOE's influence in Latin and Central America, a circumstance that may fit comfortably into the region's political culture but has also had clear drawbacks.

The Spanish Socialist role in the SI encouraged the PSOE's interest in Central American issues. As noted in chapter 1, the PSOE had been taken under the wing of the SPD in the early 1970s, receiving extensive organizational and financial assistance for itself and its trade union affiliate from the SPD and its foundation, the Friedrich Ebert Stiftung. Drawing on the success it had in Spain (and in neighboring Portugal) during the mid-1970s, the SPD viewed the Iberian transitions to democracy as models for what might occur to the authoritarian regimes of the Western Hemisphere. Interested in expanding the European Socialist and Social Democratic presence in the region, the SPD and Willy Brandt in particular urged the PSOE and Felipe González to become involved in the region. As vice president of the SI and head of its Committee for the Defense of the Nicaraguan Revolution, González visited the region on numerous occasions (a dozen times by 1982), thereby becoming one of the architects of European Socialist involvement in the region.

The PSOE had entered the Central American scene in the late 1970s as the winds of revolution swept through the region. It viewed the Sandinista seizure of power in July 1979 as an opportunity for profound and positive changes in the regional balance of power. Flush with ideological zeal, the PSOE adopted a harsh and strident rhetoric, one that is worth recalling, if only to contrast it with González's more prudent statements in subsequent years. Convinced that the Salvadorean guerrillas' "final offensive" in January 1981 would succeed, the PSOE endorsed SI President Willy Brandt and Secretary General Bernt Carlsson's statement calling for "revolutionary change" in El Salvador, now that "all attempts at peaceful political change had been blocked by violence and fraud."[11] About this time, an article in the weekly *El Socialista* was apocalyptic in describing the situation:

> Two forces are in tension against each other: the imperialist line which acts in alliance with local reaction and tries to keep the region within the mold of dependent capital development, keeping it as an object of intense financial and economic exploitation; and the progressive, anti-imperialist line which understands clearly the incompatibility between the interests of national development and those which seek to conserve national dependence with respect to the monopolies.[12]

Salvadorean Christian Democratic (PDC) leader José Napoleón Duarte was also the target of biting attacks. One article in *El Socialista* referred to him as "a dangerous intriguer"; another declared that "[within the PDC] there remain only the right-wing sectors, those led by Napoleón Duarte."[13]

The tenor of Socialist statements soon became more moderate. By late 1981, PSOE leaders no longer anticipated or even desired an insurgent victory in El Salvador; instead, the focus was on encouraging negotiated settlements throughout the region. In line with this approach, the PSOE helped draft an April 1982 SI Bureau statement that referred to the FMLN-FDR coalition as "an important political representative force" but urged only that it participate in any "comprehensive political solution."[14] Alongside this renewed emphasis on negotiations in El Salvador also came a more nuanced appreciation of Duarte. *El Socialista* did refer to the March 1982 legislative elections in El Salvador as a "farce," but neither Duarte nor his supporters' democratic credentials were openly challenged, and the analysis of the elections themselves showed a more nuanced assessment of the conflict and of the limits to popular backing for the insurgents.[15]

With respect to the Sandinistas, too, a more skeptical view had also begun to prevail. González had dealt frequently with members of the FSLN Directorate and had become convinced that many of them were eager to fuel a "siege mentality" in an attempt to consolidate control over Nicaraguan society. Although critical of the Reagan administration's policy toward Nicaragua, he had nevertheless become quite concerned with the pattern of harassment against opposition leaders in labor and the Church, media censorship, the adoption of economic measures directed against the middle class, the FSLN's Marxist-Leninist orientation and rhetoric, and the growing presence of Cuban and East German security personnel. In an early display of concern after a trip to Managua in late 1981 (shortly after the arrest of several business leaders), he and former Venezuelan president Carlos Andrés Pérez urged Willy Brandt to show the SI's displeasure with the FSLN by not inviting it to attend an upcoming SI meeting in Caracas.

**The Socialist Government's
Central American Policy**

The Socialists entered office in December 1982, having clearly moderated their views on Central American issues but still firmly "committed to [developing] a presence and [undertaking] resolute action on the Iberoamerican continent."[16] With respect to Central America, in particular, González wanted to convoke a "mini-Helsinki" conference for which Spain would act as host.[17] He wanted to add a European dimension to the Contadora process and to involve Cuba in the negotiations. Because González and his foreign minister believed that the solution to the Central American imbroglio involved mediating a rapprochement between the United States and Cuba, they attached special importance to the latter's participation. In their opinion, the Castro regime had lost the enthusiasm for revolution in Central America that had influenced its policies through the late 1970s and into the early 1980s. Outflanked by Nicaragua and the more radical elements in the Salvadorean guerrilla movement, Castro now wanted to avoid actions that might provoke an outright U.S. intervention in the region, fearing that this would render Cuba more vulnerable to both U.S. and Soviet pressure.

In the months after González made his mini-Helsinki proposal, there was a great flurry of Spanish diplomatic activity regarding Central America. At this time, and perhaps to secure the support of other Western European governments, Foreign Minister Fernando Morán also offered a plan for Franco-Spanish collaboration in the region.[18] Thomas Enders, the U.S. assistant secretary of state for Latin America, also visited Madrid in early 1983, and while presenting the two-track Reagan administration policy (combining military pressure with a search for a negotiated settlement), he apparently queried the González government about its willingness to facilitate conversations between the contending parties. Adding a final dimension to the Spanish government's efforts were its intensified consultations with Mexico and Cuba. Cuban Vice Premier Carlos Rafael Rodríguez came to Madrid during these hectic weeks, making an unscheduled technical stopover on his return from a trip to Eastern Europe. González also became personally involved in the discussions, meeting with both

Cuban Foreign Minister Isidoro Malmierca and Cuban Communist Party (PCC) Political Bureau member and Castro confidant Armando Hart.

The mini-Helsinki initiative was brief; by March 1983 it had come to a disappointing end. Thereafter, the Spanish government opted for a more discreet and less intense engagement in the region. Enders had come under fire from within the administration (it would appear that both personal and political conflicts led to his replacement in May 1983; he subsequently became ambassador to Madrid), and the U.S. government soon conveyed its lack of enthusiasm for the Spanish offer to mediate the long-standing conflict with Cuba or to involve itself in Central American negotiations. But it was not only the United States that discouraged González from pursuing his project. Other nations with stakes in the region (including the Contadora countries) publicly supported the Spanish initiative; privately and unofficially, however, a number of governments viewed Spain as an interloper and distrusted both its instincts and objectives in Central America. González soon realized this and, having concluded that there was neither a quick nor easy solution to the crisis in the region, determined that discretion was the better part of valor. "We were going to be bogged down," he said, comparing the probable fate of a formal Spanish initiative to what happened to the French Socialist government after it signed the August 1981 declaration with Mexico, which recognized a state of belligerency in El Salvador.[19] Thereafter, he announced, his government would "collaborate" with any efforts to negotiate a settlement, but it would not "mediate."[20]

This would remain the general line of the Spanish Socialist government with respect to Central America in subsequent years. It would eschew direct or unilateral engagement in the region, focusing its energies instead on rallying multilateral support (whether through joint action by EC governments or through common initiatives pursued by European Socialist or Social Democratic parties) for regional initiatives. The Spanish Council of Ministers explicitly endorsed Contadora in April 1983 in a statement declaring that the Central American crisis could be surmounted by a "change in social structures and the establishment of liberties and the principles of a representative system," and thereafter the government spared no effort in promoting the Contadora formula.[21] The participant governments received the prestigious *Príncipe de Asturias* award, and within European Community councils (Spain became an EC member in January 1986), Spain became its unstinting advocate. At the European level, the Spanish government worked diligently behind the scenes, helping to organize the first Contadora–European Community summit in September 1984 and playing a similarly active role in the more recent ones.

These efforts underscored Spain's commitment to playing an active role in formulating and implementing European Community policies toward Central (and Latin) America, but they also revealed the limits to Spanish and European activism in the region. The first EC Foreign Ministers' meeting in Costa Rica only agreed in principle to increase the Community's aid level to Central America; even so, the $45 million they mentioned was risible.[22] A similar inertia was visible when the Spanish proposed that the EC increase its quotas for bananas, coffee, and sugar imported from Caribbean and Central American countries: here the objection was that such a measure would require extensive renegotiations of the aid and tariff provisions of the Lomé conventions. Spain unveiled its own regional cooperation plan in 1984, providing approximately $1.5 million for projects in Costa Rica, Honduras, and Nicaragua. By 1987, despite a nearly quadrupled budget, Spain funded fewer than 200 *cooperantes* (volunteer workers) in the region.[23]

Chastened by its experience with the mini-Helsinki initiative, the Spanish government began to lower its profile in Central America after 1983. Subsequent developments in the region further encouraged it in this direction. In El Salvador, there was an evident stalemate in the war. If the army could not win, neither could the FMLN guerrillas significantly extend their base of support and operations. When the latter shifted to urban terrorism and kidnapping in mid-1985, relations with the PSOE worsened. The Spanish Socialists began grudgingly to recognize José Napoleón Duarte's popular support. In May 1984, González joined Willy Brandt, Carlos Andrés Pérez, and José Peña Gómez in sending Duarte a congratulatory letter on his victory in the Salvadorean presidential elections, and the Spanish government then dispatched a delegation headed by Council of State President Antonio Hernández Gil to attend his inauguration. A friend of Duarte's, the respected Spanish Christian Democratic leader Fernando Alvarez de Miranda, was appointed ambassador (paralleling the French Socialist nomination of Alain Rouquié) in late 1984. Most significant, Duarte made an official visit to Madrid in November 1985, which paved the way for regular exchanges between the two governments. Thereafter, the Spanish government also approved an aid package for El Salvador with provisions for cooperation in the education and health fields as well for training judicial personnel.

Notwithstanding its diplomatic recognition of El Salvador, the Spanish government did not abandon either its contacts with the FMLN guerrillas or its support for their allies in the civilian opposition, the Democratic Revolutionary Front (FDR), an umbrella coalition headed by Guillermo Ungo. Contacts with guerrillas continued because the Spanish government believed that eventually there would have to be a negotiated settlement in El Salvador, one in which the FMLN had to be included. Given this perspective, then, it was no surprise that the Spanish ambassador to El Salvador accompanied several guerrilla leaders on their flight into the country for the October 1984 negotiations in La Palma. The Spanish Socialists were also unwilling to abandon Guillermo Ungo and his civilian supporters in the Revolutionary Nationalist Movement (Movimiento Nacional Revolucionario or MNR). Like many of its European counterparts, the PSOE was perfectly aware of his weak political position—his dependence on and vulnerability to the FMLN. While suggesting to Ungo that he mark his distance from the guerrillas, the PSOE continued to support him out of loyalty and because, in the Socialist view, there would be no chance for a moderate Left ever to develop in El Salvador without the political and physical survival of Ungo (and others such as Rubén Zamora).

With respect to Nicarauga, too, the Spanish Socialists adopted a more cautious approach. Although the government continued to extend economic aid and credits to Nicaragua (in April 1983, for example, the Banco Exterior de España granted a $45 million line of credit for equipment and spare parts), González became more forthright in voicing his disenchantment with developments in Nicaragua. In a May 1983 interview with the Mexican newspaper *Unomasuno*, he bluntly warned the Sandinistas that continued Spanish support depended on whether they maintained "the original plan of the process."[24] A few weeks later, he prevailed on Brandt to join him and Carlos Andrés Pérez in sending a public letter to the FSLN, warning that it risked losing international support if elections were not soon held and democratic norms established in Nicaragua.

Among the events that contributed to the PSOE's disenchantment with the FSLN was the October 1983 arrest by Costa Rican police of a commando team (belonging to the Basque terrorist organization Euskadi ta Askatasuna or ETA) whose plan it was to assassinate contra leader Edén Pastora.[25] The Nicaraguan government quickly denied any connection with ETA, which was just at this moment stepping up its attacks on military and police targets in Spain, and dispatched Interior Minister Tomás Borge to Madrid. Neither Borge's public nor his private denials of any Nicaraguan involvement with ETA or knowledge about its activities were especially credible. Subsequently, the Ministry of the Interior leaked a document confirming Basque terrorists' long-standing ties with the Sandinistas. ETA members had fought in the war against Nicaraguan President Anastasio Somoza, and intelligence reports noted the existence of two training camps run by the organization in the outskirts of Managua.

The documents captured after the October 1983 Grenada invasion – specifically the ones dealing with the SI – also furnished Spanish officials with a rare and troubling glimpse of how the FSLN and Cuban Communist Party officials colluded to exploit what one document described as "the sharp divisions" within the SI on Central American issues.[26] Responding to these developments, the PSOE hosted a little-publicized meeting of various European members of the SI whose agenda included discussion of ways to tighten membership requirements so groups of Marxist-Leninist persuasion would not be admitted to the organization.[27] PSOE leaders also quietly backed the French Socialists when they demanded an inquiry into the New Jewel Movement's membership in the SI.

González and other PSOE leaders were also unhappy with the assurances that they had received from the Sandinistas about the upcoming presidential and legislative elections. Having urged the FSLN to move the date of these elections forward and to undertake negotiations with the opposition to ensure its participation, the Socialists became concerned in early 1984 by the lack of progress. A few months later, after publicly urging that credence be given to Nicaraguan assurances about these elections, the Spanish government communicated its displeasure with the pace of the negotiations by discreetly recalling the technical personnel it had sent to advise the Sandinistas on election procedures. Encouraged when the Nicaraguan government actually scheduled elections for November, the PSOE closely followed the negotiations between the FSLN and opposition leaders. During the fall, when a positive outcome was in doubt, González urged the Sandinistas to allow a brief postponement to have time to hammer out an agreement with the opposition. Accordingly, Spanish Socialist leaders actively participated in the negotiations between opposition leader Arturo Cruz and FSLN *comandante* Bayardo Arce at the October 1984 SI meeting in Rio de Janeiro.

These efforts were ultimately unsuccessful. Arce, who had been taken aback when Cruz offered to consider a specific set of Sandinista proposals on the conduct of the election campaign, categorically rejected a proposal that the deadline be extended for negotiations and for filing in the presidential election.[28] In adopting this position, the FSLN gambled that most European Socialist parties, concerned lest they be perceived as providing further ammunition to the Reagan administration, would accept the legitimacy of the elections, even without Cruz's participation.

The Spanish government unenthusiastically accepted Daniel Ortega's election to the presidency with 67 percent of the vote (the election, declared the Foreign Ministry's director general for Iberoamerican affairs, "might be a factor for democratization in the future"),[29] but González pointedly declined an invitation to attend Daniel Ortega's inauguration. When Ortega visited Madrid in May 1985 and asked for increased aid, the Spanish leader not only refused but, shortly after Ortega left, suspended further credits owing to Nicaragua's failure to pay earlier debts.[30]

Additional evidence illustrating the strains between the Spanish Socialists and the FSLN during this period was the PSOE's intensified contacts with the Nicaraguan opposition. At an official level, these were limited to conversations with civilian opponents of the Sandinistas. Vice Prime Minister Alfonso Guerra met with representatives of the opposition Coordinadora, and embassy personnel in Managua remained in touch, for example, with the Social Christian Party. Other, more controversial, contacts were pursued in the party's name. In August 1984, the Organizational and International Secretaries Guillermo Galeote and Elena Flores (respectively) met with exiled opposition and contra representatives in Costa Rica. This followed González's own decision to meet with Edén Pastora in his capacity as PSOE first secretary in late summer 1984 at party headquarters in Madrid and again during a subsequent vacation trip to Venezuela.[31]

Although these efforts and similar initiatives were criticized by both the Sandinistas and the Socialist left wing, they formed part of González's broader effort to eschew direct involvement as a "mediator" but to present Spain as an "honest broker" on the Nicaraguan question. To facilitate negotiations between the Sandinistas and the opposition, several Spanish efforts were undertaken without great fanfare and only after consulting with other European countries as well as with Central American governments. For example, the Spanish embassy in Managua hosted talks between the FSLN and representatives of the Nicaraguan Social Christian Party in late 1985.[32]

Despite disapproval of the Sandinistas' internal course, González and his associates remained adamant in their opposition to the Reagan administration's policies in the region, particularly toward Nicaragua. Their objections were twofold. One dimension was moral-ethical. In the PSOE's view, the United States had no right to intervene in Nicaragua's internal affairs; in this respect, its policies in the region were indistinguishable from those of the Soviet Union in Afghanistan. The second objection had a more tactical-political foundation. If the U.S. objective was to encourage the democratization of Nicaraguan society, González believed, its policies were counterproductive. A confrontational posture only encouraged the Marxist-Leninist elements in the FSLN to adopt more radical policies internally and to deepen their involvement with Cuba and the Soviet Union.

González and those around him harbored very few illusions about the Sandinistas. González's conversations with FSLN leaders (Daniel Ortega and Sergio Ramírez come readily to mind) had been blunt and direct, but there was no alternative to negotiating a settlement with the FSLN. In power since 1979, the Sandinistas were well entrenched; the contras had given little evidence of being able to topple them. The only force capable of accomplishing this was the United States, whose intervention would be not only wrong but stupid.

The decisive and, indeed, dominant voice in Spanish

policy-making toward Central America has belonged to Felipe González. Several institutions and individuals, primarily the Foreign Ministry, the Institute for Iberoamerican Cooperation (ICI), and the PSOE's International Department have provided him with support in the elaboration and execution of Spain's Central American policy. Coordination has been provided by the prime minister's office in the Moncloa Palace, where Juan Antonio Yañez (whose brief is foreign policy) and his deputy for Latin American affairs, José Rodríguez Spiteri, have served as a combination national security council and policy-planning staff.

The Foreign Ministry's influence on Central American questions has varied, depending on both the interest González displays about a specific initiative and his relations with the foreign minister. Relations between González and his first foreign minister, Fernando Morán, were never close. Their personality and generational differences became entangled with divergent approaches in foreign policy. Morán held to a more traditional, nationalist perspective that also had a neutralist and, to a certain degree, anti-American thrust. González, on the other hand, gave primacy to Spanish economic modernization and became increasingly convinced that seeking good relations with the United States was unavoidable (and even desirable). Following the failure of the mini-Helsinki proposal and of the Franco-Spanish initiative in early 1983, Morán's role on Central American issues declined.

His successor, Francisco Fernández Ordoñez, was an able technocrat whose foreign policy views and moderate instincts dovetailed more nearly with those of González. After taking office in mid-1985, he staked out a somewhat more active presence in the foreign policy-making scheme but was also careful not to overplay the Spanish hand. Fernández Ordoñez's first major initiative in Central America—a trip in January 1986 to Vinicio Cerezo's inauguration as Guatemalan president and then a sojourn through various other countries in the region—represented a modest *relanzamiento* (relaunching) of Spanish policy.[33] It did not involve an active effort to "mediate" but was designed primarily as an *acto de presencia* (act of presence) and as a signal of Spanish support for the still tenuous process of democratization in Guatemala.

Within the Foreign Ministry, the director general for Iberoamerican affairs provided the main input on Central American issues. During her tenure, Mercedes Rico (later named ambassador to Costa Rica and subsequently director general for human rights) earned a reputation as a tough-minded and informed analyst.[34] Her successor Juan Pablo de la Iglesia (and his deputy José Antonio Martínez de Villarreal) did not develop a similar influence. A more recent appointee to this post was Yago Pico de la Coaña, a former ambassador to Nicaragua, who had a much more active profile and was increasingly relied on by the Moncloa staff.

Two other institutions have influenced Spain's Central American policy. One is the ICI – the organization responsible for administering most Spanish development aid to Latin America. Because it lacks an adequate budget and its bureaucracy is cumbersome and inefficient, ICI is unlikely soon to match the influence of the SPD's Friedrich Ebert Stiftung in Latin America.[35] On the other hand, its director, Luis Yañez, is close to González. Not only does his brother serve in the Moncloa, but his own links to the Spanish prime minister go back to the early 1970s when they were both leaders of the clandestine PSOE organization in Seville.

The other institutional focus of influence on Central American issues resided in the PSOE International Department whose international secretary since 1986 was Elena Flores. Her influence expanded over the past five years as her responsibilities shifted from the coordination of visits and the collection of information to a much more active participation in the formulation of Spanish initiatives. Although Flores certainly could not take exclusive credit for it, her heightened personal role was not divorced from her party's growing weight in European Socialist and Socialist

International councils. There, the PSOE had become a major force in discussions about Central America, a fact underscored when it hosted the European Socialist caucus in 1984 after the Grenada invasion as well as the meeting between the FSLN and four European parties in early 1987.[36]

Conclusion

After Felipe González became prime minister in December 1982, both Spanish policy toward Central America and the centrality of his role in its formulation remained remarkably consistent. He shifted away from supporting revolutionary movements in the region earlier than either the leaders of the SPD or the other Northern European Social Democratic parties. Having embarked on several initiatives early in his mandate, however, González settled for a more modest agenda over the next several years. The phase of less intense engagement lasted until early 1986 when he resolved the conundrum over Spanish membership in NATO. Once he won the government-sponsored referendum on this question, González could reclaim a more activist dimension for his foreign policy.[37]

The Spanish Socialists rekindled their Central American engagement in late 1986 and early 1987, just as a regional peace initiative sponsored by Costa Rican President Oscar Arias was getting off the ground. Emboldened by this development, González and the PSOE reentered the scene, pressing for a resumption of the dialogue between the FSLN and the opposition as well as an improvement in Costa Rican-Nicaraguan relations. These were the principal items discussed at a meeting that the Spanish Socialists hosted in February 1987 attended by the FSLN and various European Socialist parties. Along with the latter, the PSOE held out the prospect of improved relations and greater support but called on the Sandinistas to lift the state of emergency, to reopen the newspaper *La Prensa*, and to undertake negotiations with the opposition.[38] The PSOE and the other parties were also emphatic about the issue of Nicaraguan relations with Costa Rica, echoing the PLN's demand that the complaint before the International Court of Justice be withdrawn in exchange for tighter restrictions on contra exile activity. A subsequent agreement on this question was announced at the SI's council meeting in April.[39]

As the Arias Plan picked up steam and led to the Esquipulas II Agreement in August 1987, the pace of Spanish diplomatic activity intensified in Central America. The Spanish government provided facilities for a meeting (unsuccessful at the time) between Guatemalan officials and representatives of the unified guerrilla command known as the Unidad Revolucionaria Nacional Guatemalteca (URNG).[40] Spain also became prominently engaged in discussions over Panama. Once the U.S. indictment of Panamanian strongman Manuel Noriega was announced, Spanish officials discussed offering him asylum if the United States promised not to seek his extradition.[41]

Nicaragua was at the center of Spanish Socialist activity. González did not make his long-announced official visit to the area (only in March 1988 did he take a "vacation" in Costa Rica), but other Spanish officials traveled to the region. As both a concession and an inducement to Nicaragua, Alfonso Guerra went to Managua in November 1987, becoming the highest-ranking European official to visit there since Somoza's overthrow in 1979. Like many of his activities in Spain, Guerra's mission had a decided double edge. On the one hand, he reassured the PSOE's leftist constituency (and the Sandinistas) by insisting that, among the Central American countries, Nicaragua had taken the "major initiative" in the peace process.[42] On the other hand, he undoubtedly delivered a message that González and the Spanish government had been preaching for some time: the moment had come for direct negotiations with the contras.

Once begun, these negotiations made it possible for Nicaraguan President Daniel Ortega to visit Madrid in Jan-

uary 1988 during a more general European tour.[43] His trip
provided him with a diplomatic boost, but he was less successful in persuading González to sign on to the International Verification Commission envisioned under the Esquipulas II Agreement. Careful lest he be burned by an
outcome that he could neither predict nor control, González
demurred and agreed to the idea only in principle. Among
other conditions, he insisted that, upon concluding a regional cease-fire, all Central American governments would
have to acquiesce to such a Spanish role.[44]

3

French Socialism:
The Politics of *Beaux Gestes*
Reconsidered

The French Socialist Party (PS) has been another European actor whose views and behavior toward the Central American crisis merit careful consideration. France's
role in the alliance and in European politics as well as the
Socialist Party's domestic and international influence have
added a special dimension to the party's engagement in the
region.

Tensions in Central America had dramatically increased
in the early 1980s, just as the Socialists, who had been out of
power in France for more than two decades, were on the
verge of assuming governmental responsibilities. François
Mitterrand's victory in the May 1981 presidential election
and the subsequent PS landslide in June's National Assembly elections raised many questions about the future direction of French foreign policy and the possible areas of confrontation with the United States.[1]

French socialism has had a strong ideological tradition.
Since the onset of the postwar era, its foreign policy perspectives have oscillated, moving from "ideological intransigence" in the late 1940s and toward *atlantisme* by the
1960s.[2] Closely identified with the Fourth Republic's policies and institutional arrangements, the Socialist Party
(still called the Section Française de l'Internationale

Ouvrière or SFIO) only slowly adjusted to the emerging foreign policy consensus that Gaullism forged during the 1960s.

Reinvigorated in the early 1970s under the leadership of Mitterrand, the PS adopted a sharply "neutralist" program. Critical of the conservative thrust that animated Gaullist doctrine, the Socialists nevertheless shared its advocacy of France's unique historical mission. Intertwining nationalism with socialism, the PS saw France as "capable of aspiring to world-wide influence." More than "a middle power," France under PS leadership would effect both "a real transition to socialism in the developed world" and a "break in the international capitalist order."[3] France had special qualifications for this task. As Jean-Pierre Cot, a prominent Socialist who was for a time minister for development and cooperation, retrospectively put it: "François Mitterrand's engagement [with the Third World] connects to the tradition of 1789, to the conviction that France, charged with a message by History, should help to sow it throughout the world."[4]

Supporting an "anti-imperialist European strategy," the Socialists called for a radical transformation of the international economic order and the generation of new forms of internationalism based on solidarity with oppressed peoples and countries.[5] In this scheme, the United States was cast as a more dangerous and insidious opponent than the Soviet Union because it threatened French sovereignty through multiple economic and political encroachments and, almost as noxiously, was the purveyor of an international consumerist and philistine culture.[6]

By the time the Socialists took power in 1981, they had modulated some of their earlier, more extreme formulations, especially on East-West issues. In 1972, for example, the PS program had placed the Soviet Union and the United States in the same category (both were "partners in the common exercise of a double hegemony" over Europe) and warned against how NATO "tied its signatories to American imperialism."[7] Later in the decade, the *Projet Socialiste* referred to the Atlantic Alliance as "a necessary counter-weight to Soviet power in Europe," and Mitterrand, whose personal authority in the PS was on a par with that of Felipe González in the Spanish PSOE, had begun to refer to the "established Soviet superiority" in Europe.[8]

This French Socialist concern with Soviet intentions and capabilities intensified in subsequent years, sym-bolically culminating in the occasion of Mitterrand's ap-pearance before the West German Bundestag in January 1983 – while an election campaign was under way in West Germany. At the time, in a speech that could only be inter-preted as a vote of "no confidence" in the SPD, he bluntly warned Germans to resist neutralist temptations and to retain strong ties with the Atlantic Alliance.[9]

On Third World issues, however, the PS retained a more radical and utopian flavor, promising to oppose the two su-perpowers' hegemonic efforts and recast French relations with developing countries in the direction of greater "soli-darity." During their first year in office, the Socialists called for numerous developmental initiatives, among them a "planetary new deal" to develop the countries of the South, the creation of an international energy agency, the restruc-turing of lending agencies such as the World Bank and the International Monetary Fund (IMF), and a worldwide agreement on the stabilization of commodity prices.[10]

The Roots of French Socialist Central American Policy

Socialist Central American policy evolved within a general framework whose major points of reference were the (par-tial) acceptance of the Gaullist assertion of France's right and duty to point the way to all nations, the advocacy of Socialist internationalism for the Third World, and a con-cern for maintaining the East-West strategic balance, espe-cially in Europe. France and its Socialists approached Cen-tral America from a different perspective than did Spain and the PSOE. Neither the country nor the party had an especially intense cultural or historical connection with Central America. Nor did they have a recent experience of transition to democracy that they wanted to share with the region.

French Socialist engagement with Central America would develop for other reasons. There was, in the first place, their identification with France's sense of *mission civilisatrice*. Former President Charles de Gaulle had evoked this sentiment in his conservative nationalist efforts to pursue a path independent of the two superpowers. He saw in Third World countries natural partners in alliance with whom France could recover its "dignity," reassert its sense of purpose and individuality, and weaken the reigning bipolar logic of the international system. For him and his successors, France's privileged arena of Third World engagement would continue to be Africa, yet Latin America, which he visited twice during the 1960s, was still important, if only because it provided manifold symbolic opportunities to irritate the United States.

Enthusiastic custodians of the 1789 revolution's legacy, the Socialists offered a more "progressive" rationale for engagement with the Third World generally and Latin America in particular. The region had risen on the French Socialist horizon after Salvador Allende's election to the presidency in Chile. Far more than elsewhere in Western Europe, his death and the overthrow of the Popular Unity coalition had struck close to home in France. Régis Debray, for one, drew an explicit analogy between what happened in Chile and what might occur in a France ruled by the *union de la gauche*.[11] Sharing these views was Mitterrand who had known Allende personally, visited him in 1971, and saw himself embarked on a similarly perilous path.[12] Chilean events drew other prominent French Socialists (among them, Danielle Mitterrand and Pierre Joxe) toward engagement with Latin American affairs. They developed their own network of contacts in the region and, more important, did not hesitate to use their influence with party leader Mitterrand.

Before coming to power in May 1981, the French Socialists had frequently reaffirmed their support for revolutionary movements in Central America. In April 1981, Mitterrand had declared that El Salvador "was a typical case of people's revolt against the excessive domination of the power of wealth and political dictatorship."[13] The revolutionaries there were not natural adversaries of the West; they were forced into this position by the logic of the situation. They were nationalists first and Communists second, or perhaps not at all. In a similar vein, PS First Secretary Lionel Jospin insisted: "The problems of armed struggle would not be raised in that country if Mr. Duarte's regime accepted political pluralism, the expression of opinions and the existence of parties."[14] Concerning Nicaragua, too, the perspective was one of strong solidarity. The 1980 *Projet Socialiste* promised it "substantial aid" as a newly "liberated country," and Claude Cheysson (the future foreign minister who was then an EC commissioner) had been influential in persuading the European Community to dispatch food and medical aid to the Sandinistas even before Anastasio Somoza's downfall.

The Socialist Government's Central American Policy

During their first year in government, Mitterrand and his colleagues pursued a Latin American policy that Guy Hermet has perceptively called the politics of the *beau geste*.[15] The early symbolic gestures included giving Salvador Allende's widow a place of honor at his inaugural and appointing Régis Debray as a personal adviser. During a subsequent October 1981 speech in Mexico city, Mitterrand stressed his administration's revolutionary attachments:

> To all combatants for liberty, France sends its message
> of hope. She sends her salute to men, women and even

children who . . . in this moment fall throughout the
world for a noble ideal. Salutations to the humiliated,
to the emigrés, to the exiles in their own lands who
want to live, to live free. . . . To all France says: Cour-
age! Liberty shall overcome.[16]

Two gambits rounded out the ambitious French Socialist agenda toward Central America. The first occurred in
August 1981 when France issued a joint declaration with
Mexico recognizing a "state of belligerency" in El Salvador
and identifying the insurgent FDR-FMLN as "a representative political force ready to take on the attendant responsibilities and exercise the attendant rights of governing."[17]
The second began its gestation during Nicaraguan Foreign
Minister Miguel d'Escoto's visit to Paris in July 1981 and
continued during Cheysson's visit to Nicaragua that same
month. After consultations with President Mitterrand and
his advisers Pierre Bérégovoy (secretary general of the Elysée staff) and Régis Debray, the two countries signed a
contract in December 1981. Described as involving "defensive weapons," it included 2 patrol boats, 2 Alouette-3 heli-
copters, and 700 air-to-surface rockets.[18]

Undertaken after extensive consultations with Mexico
(to whom France had looked, ever since the middle of the
nineteenth century, as its privileged interlocutor in the region), these initiatives had been designed to enhance
French prestige and margin for maneuver, but their consequences were exactly the opposite of what had been intended. The initiatives provoked strongly negative reactions
from the United States. Secretary of State Alexander M.
Haig and Secretary of Defense Caspar Weinberger bluntly
conveyed their dismay about the arms sale to their French
counterparts.[19] White House aide Michael Deaver also traveled to Paris to meet with Jacques Attali, Mitterrand's clos-
est adviser in the Elysée, informing him that the Reagan
administration considered France's actions in Central
America as "hostile" and "irresponsible."[20]

Latin American reaction to the Franco-Mexican declaration was almost as intense. Only a few days after it had been issued, the foreign ministers from nine Latin American countries (among them, Colombia and Venezuela) issued a joint statement condemning "[this] interfere[nce] in the internal affairs of El Salvador."[21] Venezuela pressed the issue even further, recalling its ambassador from Paris for consultations.

The vehemence of these reactions resulted in a partial French withdrawal from the Central American region.[22] Mitterrand visited the United States in March 1982, and shortly thereafter the government announced it would delay shipment of the arms for "technical" reasons. The French government completed delivery of $18 million worth of trucks, helicopters, and planes by midsummer 1983, but then consistently turned down every Nicaraguan request for more arms.[23]

Two years into Mitterrand's mandate, French incursions into the region became more discreet and episodic than before. The French government continued to provide Nicaragua with economic aid and credits (an agreement signed in November 1984 called for a $1.75 million grant for technical cooperation, $15 million in loans under favorable conditions, and the continuation of 20,000 tons of annual food aid).[24] Between July and September 1984, France also hosted border talks between Costa Rica and Nicaragua.[25]

The French government undertook these initiatives without great fanfare, however, because it was eager to avoid embarrassments similar to those resulting from earlier efforts. Tactical considerations were not the only reason for disengagement, however. Events in Grenada (Maurice Bishop's overthrow by an apparently pro-Soviet faction and the subsequent U.S. invasion) had a clear impact on French Socialist perspectives. Like most other Socialist-led European governments (the exception was Portugal), it had disapproved of the U.S. action, but the Socialists were not unaware of the trouble brewing within the New Jewel Movement, and they were acutely conscious of the dangerous consequences a radicalized Caribbean would have for the

French "overseas territories" in Guadaloupe and Martinique. In this respect, the Grenadian documents indicating extensive contacts between the New Jewel Movement, the FSLN, and the Cuban Communist Party represented an additional concern. Within the Socialist International, the French PS now increasingly joined a nascent "southern European bloc" that adopted more critical perspectives toward revolutionary change in Central America.

Further contributing to the change in French Socialist tone were growing doubts that the Nicaraguans would remain faithful to the "original" promise of maintaining political pluralism, a mixed economy, and nonalignment. The first public sign of displeasure came on the occasion of Nicaraguan President Daniel Ortega's visit in July 1982, when Mitterrand pointedly urged that government to maintain "genuine nonalignment," but public and private admonitions directed at the Sandinistas intensified in subsequent years.[26] French Socialist criticism focused particularly on the FSLN's manipulation of the promised presidential and legislative elections. Meeting with Ortega at the funeral of Soviet General Secretary Yuri Andropov in early 1984, Cheysson insisted that such elections be held by the end of the year. They were so scheduled, but not to the satisfaction of the French government, which, emphasizing both the importance it attached to "free elections" and the obstacles placed in the way of the Nicaraguan opposition, declined a Nicaraguan invitation to send observers to the November 1984 contest.[27]

After 1982, the most prominent efforts undertaken by the French Socialist government involved its unsuccessful efforts to persuade the Spanish government in early 1983 to engage in a joint initiative in Central America, and the offer Cheysson made to Colombian President Belisario Betancur indicating that France would join a multinational (Latin American and European) force in removing the mines planted in Nicaraguan ports by U.S.-backed rebels.[28] Neither of these initiatives prospered; in the instance involving Spain, the reasons are discussed in chapter 2. As for Cheysson's offer, there is good reason to believe that the French government did not expect it to materialize, particularly because others would have had to join in the venture.

In the post-1982 period, the French Socialists also reappraised their policy toward El Salvador. PS First Secretary Lionel Jospin had labeled its March 1982 legislative elections a facade, but many Socialists (including Jospin during a subsequent trip to the United States) soon admitted that they had misjudged the left opposition's base of support as well as underestimated popular backing for Duarte and his Christian Democratic Party.[29]

The French Socialist government confronted several dilemmas in rebalancing its policy toward El Salvador. It had taken a formal position in the August 1981 Franco-Mexican declaration, and for reasons of prestige it did not want to be perceived as changing course. Neither did the French Socialists wish to forsake Guillermo Ungo. Like their counterparts in the Spanish PSOE, many prominent Socialists (from François Mitterrand on down) had developed ties of friendship with Ungo. They considered that he and his MNR offered the only chance for the emergence of a moderate Left in El Salvador. Many Socialists were, it should also be noted, unconvinced about Duarte's prospects.

The result was a slow and carefully calibrated change in policy. The PS maintained political links with Ungo and the MNR. Mitterrand received the Salvadorean in April 1984, but the government also upgraded its relations with El Salvador. In February 1983, after a two-week trip through the region, roving ambassador Antoine Blanca announced France's intention to upgrade its diplomatic relations with El Salvador by sending a chargé d'affaires, explaining further that "we are now limiting ourselves to supporting the initiatives of countries like Mexico, Colombia, Venezuela and Panama."[30] In November 1983, Cheysson met with Salvadorean Foreign Minister Fidel Chavez Mena in Paris (the first official high-level contact between the two governments), and eight months later, in July 1984, Mitterrand hosted an official visit by Duarte.[31] Finally in April 1985, the French government announced the appointment of Quai d'Orsay planning staff aide and prominent academician Alain Rouquié as ambassador to San Salvador.

The evolution in French Socialist policy toward Central America after 1982 can be explained by the confluence between changed PS perspectives (the result of having assumed and identified with national and governmental responsibilities) and other external and internal developments that conditioned the government's range of alternatives. The first year of the Socialist mandate was a period of euphoria. Mitterrand's triumph marked the end of a nearly quarter-century hiatus during which the PS had not only been in the opposition but (for much of the time) on the defensive in relation to its Communist partner. Considering these circumstances and French socialism's strong ideological tradition, no one should have been surprised either by the radical tone of the party's domestic and international programs or with initial Socialist efforts to implement some of those proposals.

Once the Socialists settled into power, it did not take long for the numerous constraints on French actions to become apparent, nor for the rather disparate perspectives on domestic and international policy to assert themselves. In the realm of foreign policy, three distinct orientations became manifest. The first approach was Eurocentric. Its exponents viewed international relations from a predominantly East-West perspective, emphasizing the effect that changes in the U.S.-Soviet strategic balance had on France and Western Europe. The second, an "enlightened developmental" approach, emphasized North-South issues and urged the government toward an "idealist-realist" synthesis that looked beyond short-term economic interests in the Third World. Such a "renovated" policy would provide a more stable foundation for the defense of French interests. While neither blind nor indifferent to U.S.-Soviet competition in the Third World, advocates of this approach wanted France to enter Third World crisis spots both to enhance its own maneuverability and to prevent the incorporation of these areas into the East-West agenda. A third approach emphasized "revolutionary solidarity" with Third World national liberation movements and causes. Some of its advocates paid little attention to East-West questions, others were carried away by elemental anti-Americanism, or by the enthusiasm of revolutionary engagement.

The initial French Socialist venture into Central America had drawn its inspiration primarily from the "idealist" perspectives provided by the "enlightened Third World" and "revolutionary solidarity" approaches. As would happen in other areas (most notably, with respect to relations with Africa and on domestic economic policy), their influence diminished over the first two years of Socialist government.[32] The more radical elements in the PS became increasingly marginal. It was less and less necessary to cater to them, all the more because their role in providing a left-wing voice for the Socialists had become less relevant with the decline in Communist fortunes. For their part, the moderate Third Worldists became convinced that there was little to be gained from confrontation with the United States. Correspondingly, there was a rise in the influence of those (soon to include Mitterrand) who wanted not only to repair the disequilibrium that had developed in the U.S.-Soviet balance but also to ensure a continued and active U.S. role in the Atlantic Alliance.

One reason for the change in French Central American policy, then, had to do with alliance issues. By mid-1982 the crisis over the deployment of tactical nuclear missiles had provoked intense debate and division in Western Europe, especially in West Germany where the growth of neutralist sentiment within the still ruling SPD threatened to undermine the solidity of German attachment to the alliance. Sensitivity to West Germany's relationship with the Atlantic Alliance cuts across most political and ideological borders in France, with widespread agreement for the proposition that a condition for France's successful pursuit of an independent foreign policy has been West Germany's firm anchor in NATO. The French Socialist government was reluctant to antagonize the United States under these conditions. The Reagan administration evidently believed firmly that vital U.S. security interests were at stake in Central America. Furthermore, interalliance bickering would weaken NATO and perhaps also encourage isolationist tendencies in the United States.

Other factors, too, contributed to the shift in French foreign policy toward Central America. One was the decline of Mexico, the country on which France had depended as its privileged interlocutor and handmaiden in the region. After 1982, however, Mexico's financial situation worsened dramatically (provoked in large measure by the impact of declining oil revenues on its ability to pay off a staggering debt) and so did its ability and willingness to become engaged in major foreign policy initiatives, especially when these promised to lead in the direction of confrontation with the United States.

A second development was related to events in El Salvador and Nicaragua, some of which have already been described in this and in the preceding chapter. Similar events include, for example, the sharply negative impact of the April 1983 murder in Managua of Melinda Anaya Montes (second-in-command of the Popular Forces of Liberation — the oldest and most hardline of the Salvadorean guerrilla groups) on the orders of the group's leader Salvador Cayetano Carpio. This was a tremendous blow to the international image of the Salvadorean Left and, especially, of the FMLN guerrilla command. It clearly demonstrated, too, Nicaragua's role as a base for guerrilla operations into El Salvador.[33] The French government was also disappointed about Nicaragua's growing alignment with the Soviet Union. Daniel Ortega had come twice to Paris, each time (in 1982 and 1985) upon returning from Moscow where the FSLN and Nicaragua's close ties with the Soviet bloc had been displayed.

A third consideration affected French foreign policy in the region. Following the Malvinas-Falklands War (1982) and the more recent instability in Grenada, the Socialist government had become concerned with the threat that "independentist" movements posed to the established order in Guadaloupe and Martinique.[34] Searching for a way to neutralize them, France had pursued contacts with Cuba, but these had ultimately proved unsatisfactory.[35] Bombings and deaths in Guadaloupe had led the Parisian-appointed *préfet* (prefect) to charge Nicaragua and Libya with providing support to revolutionaries there.[36] Officials in the Defense and Interior ministries, on guard because of developments in New Caledonia, were also keen to emphasize the threat Caribbean revolutionaries posed to French strategic interests.

The presidentialist emphasis of the French political system and the president's unassailable role as party leader determined that it was Mitterrand who gave general direction and purpose to Socialist foreign policy between 1981 and 1986.[37] His engagement in Central American issues was especially intense in late 1981 and early 1982, when he relied heavily on Régis Debray. In the aftermath of the Franco-Mexican declaration and of the U. S. reaction to the Nicaraguan arms sales, Mitterrand moved to limit his direct exposure to criticism by delegating most of the direct responsibility on Central American issues to Foreign Minister Claude Cheysson. He and the Foreign Ministry took the lead in French policy toward Central America in the post-1982 period. Mitterrand displayed a renewed interest in Central American issues after the U.S. trade embargo was declared in May 1985, publicly criticizing the action at the Venice summit. Partly because his new Foreign Minister Roland Dumas did not have a strong background in Central America, the locus of interest as well as decision making shifted from the Quai d'Orsay to the Elysée until the March 1986 legislative elections brought a conservative government headed by Jacques Chirac to power.

Mitterrand developed his own presidential style of foreign policy-making. It allowed "a cacophony of voices from his office, from a variety of ministries, and from Socialist Party circles openly to influence and even represent French foreign policy."[38] Among the independent advisers who played a role in formulating policy toward Central America, Régis Debray and Alain Rouquié should receive special mention. Debray was particularly active during the first year of the Socialist mandate, but thereafter his influence declined considerably, despite his personal friendship with Madame Mitterrand.[39] The other prominent adviser on Central American affairs was Rouquié who, as mentioned earlier, became ambassador to El Salvador in April 1985.[40] His skepticism about both Duarte's ability to control the army and seriousness in the pursuit of negotiations with the guerrillas were probably responsible for the French Socialist reluctance either to cut off relations with the FMLN-FDR or to be more supportive of the Duarte government.

The French Socialist Party did not greatly influence decision making on Central America during the period from 1981 to 1986. PS First Secretary Lionel Jospin was a close associate and loyal lieutenant of President Mitterrand. His major responsibilities were domestic: to keep PS factionalism under control and to strengthen the party's organization. Despite his participation in Socialist International Bureau meetings where Central America was discussed, he did not focus much attention on the subject. For his part, Jacques Huntzinger, who was international relations secretary until 1985 when he made way for the *rocardien* (follower of Socialist government leader Michel Rocard) Louis Le Pensec, had little active interest in Central American issues and preferred to focus on disarmament questions. That he was an intellectual with little independent base in the party did not strengthen his hand (he owed his position primarily to his relationship with Jospin and his academic expertise on East-West issues). Under him, with specific responsibility for Latin American issues, was Nicole Bourdillat; later under Le Pensec, the new *responsable* was Marie Duflo. Both attended Socialist International meetings devoted to Latin American issues, but because they were middle-level functionaries, neither had real influence in the formulation or execution of French Socialist policy toward Central America.

Party militants and some members of the PS parliamentary group became increasingly frustrated with the pragmatism the government displayed on Central American and other Third World issues. They expressed this dissatisfaction in a number of ways, none of which was particularly effective in changing the main lines of Mitterrand's foreign policy after 1982. Opposition to government policy coalesced in the National Assembly around Pierre Joxe, one of Mitterrand's oldest political supporters. This personal relationship strengthened his hand in dealing with Elysée staffers.

Under Joxe's leadership, the parliamentary group conceived of itself as akin to the party's "conscience," a role that was not entirely dysfunctional for the PS insofar as it permitted the Socialists to compete with the Communists and other groups to their Left who were sharply critical of the government. Parliamentarians established "study commissions" that acted as shadow cabinets examining the party's compliance to the Socialist program. On Central American issues, a Franco-Nicaraguan Friendship Caucus emerged in the assembly under the leadership of Jean Natiéz, a member of the left-wing Centre d'Etudes et de Recherches Socialistes (CERES). This group issued numerous declarations of solidarity with the Sandinistas, sent official delegations to Central America, and received Nicaraguan officials in Paris. A number of left-wing Socialist deputies were also active in extraparliamentary organizations opposed to U.S. policy, organizing petitions, undertaking fundraising, and organizing volunteer solidarity brigades to help build roads and schools in Nicaragua. Among the National Solidarity Committee's most prominent members were Régis Debray and Danielle Mitterrand.

The French Socialists were almost invariably critical of U.S. policies in Central America and pointedly criticized the Reagan administration in international forums, but after the initial Central American incursion in 1981–1982, they eschewed further active engagement in the region. With Mexico sidelined by its economic problems and the Miguel de la Madrid administration's effort to downplay points of friction with the United States, France lost its principal interlocutor. Although Le Pensec attended the February 1987 meeting with the FSLN in Madrid and joined in the critical chorus, by and large the French Socialists were absent from the Central American debates in the Socialist International.[41] They resented, in any case, what they perceived to be the SPD's predominance within the organization and participated in its activities more with an eye to damage control than anything else.

From their perspective as a government party through 1986, the French Socialists simply concluded that they had too many other problems (among them, mounting economic difficulties) and shared too much the Reagan administration's views on East-West issues to challenge it too directly on Central America. The substance of the French position had been aptly summarized by Cheysson in remarks before the National Assembly in February 1983:

> The government cannot follow the honorable member of Parliament when he recommends that more pressure be exerted on the Reagan Administration to make it change its policy in Central America. France can, of course, deplore the fact that the trends it promotes are not taking place as rapidly as it hopes. But rather than exert pressure, it would prefer to continue its diplomatic action with respect to Washington, which it hopes to convince.[42]

Conclusion

Neither French Socialist attitudes nor its policies toward Central America changed very much after the PS lost its parliamentary majority in March 1986. Factional struggles within the party intensified after it rejoined the opposition, and these were exacerbated by internal jockeying for position prior to the May 1988 presidential election that Mitterrand won. These conflicts did not revolve around and had little impact on foreign policy issues, however. With the subsequent formation of a Socialist-led government under Michel Rocard, the PS was ready once again to assume responsibility for French foreign policy. No changes or innovations were expected toward Central America, however. The Socialists still lacked both the instruments, the will, and perhaps the interest to pursue an activist policy in the region.

4

West German Social Democracy:
The Politics of Organized
Internationalism

No European Socialist or Social Democratic party has been more important to or influential on Central American issues during the past decade than the West German Social Democratic Party (SPD). There are several reasons why the West German Social Democrats have retained their prominence on many foreign policy issues, including those related to Central America. They were in power from 1969 to 1982 and are today the major opposition party (with 37 percent of the votes in the 1987 Bundestag elections). They have internationally prominent leaders, a well-organized party foreign policy apparatus (at the SPD's disposal is a well-financed foundation, the Friedrich Ebert Stiftung), and connections to a similarly endowed trade union movement organized around the DGB. The Social Democrats have also made persistent efforts to coordinate joint initiatives with other Socialist and Social Democratic parties within the EC and through the Socialist International.

The foreign relations of the SPD have been conditioned by the unique place that the Federal Republic of Germany holds in Western Europe and in the superpowers' strategic calculations. Although most West Germans are resigned to their country's division, the subject remains painfully alive, a constant reminder of a past Germans want to forget and of vulnerability, weakness, and dependence in the present. The *Sonderweg* tradition – a belief that Germany should pursue a third way, distinct from both East and West, with a focus on national unity and a destiny as a force in Central Europe – draws its sustenance precisely from the strength of this disquiet.

Defeated by Konrad Adenauer's CDU in a succession of postwar elections, the SPD did not enter national government until the formation of the Grand Coalition in 1966. Meanwhile, the Social Democrats experienced an important transformation.[1] In foreign policy, the SPD dropped its opposition to German rearmament and accepted Adenauer's insistence on full integration of the Federal Republic into the Atlantic Alliance. Domestically, the party made important programmatic modifications that culminated at the 1959 Bad Godesberg Congress with the elimination of references to Marxism and the espousal of a clearly reformist agenda. Entry into the Grand Coalition with the Christian Democrats and the subsequent assumption of primary governmental responsibility following the 1969 elections vindicated the Social Democrats' moderate strategy.

From the time Willy Brandt became chancellor in 1969 until his successor, Helmut Schmidt, left office in 1982, the Social Democrats – in coalition with the liberal Free Democratic Party (FDP) – presided over an unprecedented expansion in the economic and political influence of the Federal Republic of Germany. During this period, West Germany developed into an economic superpower and became the second largest exporter in the world after the United States, with its corporations investing more than DM 59 billion (through 1978) in other countries.[2] Paralleling the expansion in West German economic influence was the Federal Republic's increased political clout. In the European arena, pursuit of an assertive foreign policy led the West German government to bold initiatives on inner German relations, Eastern Europe, and the Soviet Union (*Ostpolitik*) as well as the EC. At once eager to transcend the persisting dilemma posed by Germany's own division as well as to overcome the fears that other Europeans might have about its resurgence, West Germany resembled a humble and occasionally defensive giant. Partly in response, it became the EC's leading champion.[3] Moreover, like Adenauer before him, Schmidt was an avowed Europeanist and Atlanticist. An architect of the European Monetary System (EMS), he and his government gave unswerving support to EC enlargement. Especially significant in encouraging the SPD's subsequent engagement in Latin and Central America was West Germany's role during the mid-1970s in helping to ensure the successful, peaceful transitions to democracy and the development of mass-based Socialist parties in Portugal and Spain.

Despite its evident successes from 1969 to 1982, during this period the SPD had also entered a period of flux and readjustment. Internally the party experienced severe strains as younger activists, many of whom represented the generation involved in university and other protest movements during the late 1960s, pressed the SPD to adopt more pronounced leftist positions. Indeed, by the end of Helmut Schmidt's mandate, his most vociferous critics were found not in the ranks of the opposition but in the radical wing of his own party.[4] During the 1970s, these activists' views, echoes of the socialist past with their references to pacifism, neutralism, and internationalism, were gradually, sometimes imperceptibly, assimilated into the SPD's foreign policy program.

The new SPD generation was itself a barometer for changes that had taken place in West German society. Anti-Communist sentiment had been diluted and, after it became evident that the United States did not support a "revision" of European borders but rather accepted the division of the Continent and Germany enshrined at Yalta, a more accommodationist mindset had developed with respect to the Soviet Union and Eastern Europe. By the late 1960s, the dream of reunification had been for all practical purposes abandoned, and West Germans were now compelled to define more clearly their own sense of national self-identity and nationhood. Keenly aware of their country's special status and vulnerability, West Germans were also eager to assume a voice within the European Community and in the alliance commensurate with their accomplishments.[5] For the most part, such sentiment was not rooted in anti-Americanism. Neither was it very different from the views animating many other West Europeans.

There was another side to this heightened "national" sensibility in West Germany, however, one which coincided with and contributed to the rise of the ecological and pacifist movements.[6] It profoundly affected the SPD, where those who wished to integrate the "new politics" groups into the party and its electorate slowly gained ascendance. This nationalism adhered to by many in the SPD's left wing and activists in the "new social movements" did have a sharply anti-American edge. Their advocacy of neutralist and pacifist ideas may have appeared far removed from the positions of traditional German nationalism; in reality, their arguments drew on national frustration with West (and East) Germany's dependence on and vulnerability to outside powers.[7] From this perspective, then, the two Germanies – and Europe – came to be seen as sharing in a "community of danger" for which the United States and the Soviet Union were equally responsible.[8] This perspective contributed to the neoneutralist conclusion that the two superpowers were essentially equivalent and West Germany should pursue a foreign policy line equidistant from both of them.

The Roots of SPD Central American Policy

Social Democratic engagement in Central American issues reflected both a concern for developments in the region and the SPD's coincident and more general discovery of the Third World as an arena for involvement. West German Social Democracy approached Central America from a perspective at once similar and distinct from those of its Spanish and French Socialist counterparts. Compelled to endure the travails of nearly 40 years of dictatorship, the PSOE had been late in developing an international perspective and strategy. Although the Spanish Socialists had a much keener sense of cultural and historical affinity with the Central American region and its problems, they had a much less well-articulated vision of the Third World and its role in world politics than either the SPD or PS. On the other hand, as befits parties whose lengthy histories were intertwined with their countries' international prominence and rivalry, these two parties shared a more elaborated "internationalist" vision. Whereas the French Socialists tended to cast their internationalism in the idiom of a pervasively French sense of *mission civilisatrice*, however, the SPD presented its internationalism in markedly less nationalistic terms.

The German Social Democrats considered themselves in the vanguard of the European Social Democratic movement. Because of the problematic history of German nationalism in the twentieth century and because of their own internationalist tradition, however, the SPD preferred to speak in broader pan-European terms. Further differentiating the SPD from its French and Spanish counterparts were its organizational strength and capacities. Complementing their own well-structured and well-financed party organizations were several other entities that the German Social Democrats tried to use in implementing a "party" foreign policy. Chief among these were the Friedrich Ebert Stiftung and the Socialist International.

The Friedrich Ebert Stiftung is the oldest of the German political foundations. Founded in 1925 and reestablished in 1945 after being prohibited during the Nazi era, its relationship with the SPD is informal because according to German law the foundations may not conduct political party activity. But the interpenetration between the two organizations (as between the Konrad Adenauer Stiftung and the CDU) is close. Members of its Board of Directors (chaired by Heinz Kuhn, former member of the SPD Presidium and former *Ministerpräsident* of the North Rhineland-Westphalia government) have been either party or trade union activists.[9]

What makes the Friedrich Ebert Stiftung a particularly impressive organization are its funding levels (the official budget in 1984 was DM 140 million, but this did not include private contributions given to the foundation) and the sense of long-term perspective that animates its actions. The foundation received more than DM 1.5 billion between 1970 and 1986 from the West German government, and in 1980 it used this money to finance 127 representatives overseas and to employ locals in its foreign offices.[10] Size alone gives the international department of the Friedrich Ebert Stiftung the dimensions of a small nation's foreign ministry. With respect to Latin America, more specifically, the Friedrich Ebert Stiftung has a budget of approximately $7-8 million in public funds and a smaller, undisclosed amount in private contributions.

Except for the more controversial political programs funded by the Friedrich Ebert Stiftung in Latin America, such as the training provided Sandinista leaders in 1978–1979 and the continuing financial support the foundation provides to the Instituto de Estudios del Sandinismo for the publication of books, most of the foundation's activities focus on development programs with a long-term payoff. The foundation's formal presence in Latin America did not begin until the 1960s. A collaborative effort with the Costa Rican PLN led to the creation in 1968 of the Centro de Estudios Democráticos de América Latina (CEDAL), a school to which hundreds of Latin Americans come yearly to receive political and ideological training. The Friedrich Ebert Stiftung provides financial and organizational support for branches of the Instituto Latinoamericano de Investigaciones Sociales[11] (the first branch of which had been founded in 1967 in Santiago, Chile) and for the Asociación Latinoamericana de Derechos Humanos headquartered in Quito. Among its other activities in Latin America, the foundation publishes the journal *Nueva Sociedad*, which describes itself as "open to all currents of progressive thought . . . advocat[ing] the development of political, economic and social democracy." Today, the foundation has offices in virtually all Latin American countries except Cuba and Paraguay.[12]

The SI was another vehicle the SPD (and especially the Brandt wing of the party) sought to use in pursuit of its international strategy and in reaching out to the Third World. In collaboration with other prominent European Social Democrats such as Olof Palme and Bruno Kreisky and with their respective parties, Brandt had remolded the SI and its agenda during the 1970s, making the organization less Eurocentric in focus and membership. The idea was not for the SI to become a directing center of international Social Democracy — even had this been desired, it would not have been possible. Instead it was to fulfill a no less important function as a tribune or forum where the more "international" wing of European Social Democracy could express its ideological and political points of convergence with Third World movements.

As the Third World and issues related to it became integrally involved with the Social Democratic agenda during the 1970s, three distinct orientations emerged within the SPD. The first, associated with Helmut Schmidt, Hans Apel, and George Leber, was dominant in a coalition government that also included the FDP. Theirs was a moderate orientation, very much in the mainstream of accepted Social Democratic orthodoxy as it had been enshrined at Bad Godesberg. Economically, it opposed those formulas — indexation, debt moratoria, and the like — which were at the core of Third World demands for a new international economic order.[13]

This approach generally supported U.S. foreign policy, but even when it did not, it aimed to isolate Third World conflicts from superpower rivalries. Western Europe and the Federal Republic of Germany would provide political and developmental assistance to Third World countries as a way of stabilizing their political and social situations. Achieving the latter objective necessitated, in their view, a certain openness (though certainly not naiveté) toward revolutionary movements in the Third World, with a view to dissuade their more moderate elements from alignment with the Soviet bloc. Because there were groups in the Third World with whom the United States could not, or would not, establish ties, Germany could play a useful role on behalf of the West in reaching out to them.

The second group crystallized around the former chancellor and Nobel Peace Prize laureate Willy Brandt and included among its members Egon Bahr and Uwe Holtz. They felt a much greater urgency and had a much more activist vision about North-South issues and the corresponding need for European "solidarity" with the Third World. Brandt, a man of boundless energy who had chafed at the enforced retirement that apparently awaited him after resigning as chancellor in 1974, set the tone for this group of "Eurointernationalists." Finding in the international arena a new lease on political life, he served as chairman of the Independent Commission on International Development Issues (which published the controversial volume *North-South: A Programme for Survival*) and as president of the SI. Interested in finding a way to liberate West Germany and other European countries from the superpowers' hegemonic ambitions, he looked to Third World countries and movements as natural allies in this enterprise.[14] Those who rallied around Brandt were especially active in articulating development policy, and they saw the SI as potentially important in galvanizing world public opinion in favor of global economic negotiations.[15] Egon Bahr may be said to have expressed their position on political change in the Third World when he declared:

> The SPD is for supporting liberation movements that obviously are supported by the populace or that are recognized by the United Nations as spokesmen for those concerned. These movements deserve not only humanitarian aid but also political and economic aid —
> with the consideration in mind that training which is

provided behind the battle lines often is important in discharging future responsibilities. Here we need to realize that even given a clear delineation that rules out weapons and munitions, any other commodity or any financial aid facilitates the armed struggle. But that is the point of support in a battle, to assert the hitherto-withheld human rights of the majority.[16]

This group sought to give West German foreign policy a more progressive cast. But its efforts were frustrated during the 1970s at the governmental level by Chancellor Helmut Schmidt and by the exigencies of the coalition partnership with the FDP. Eager to expand Germany and Western Europe's margin of autonomy vis-à-vis the United States and armed with a coherent ideological program that emphasized the internationalist dimension of Social Democracy, the individuals in this current devoted most of their attention to intraparty work and to the activities of the Friedrich Ebert Stiftung as well as the SI.

An even more audacious (and anti-U.S.) perspective on Third World issues was to be found among the neo-Marxist elements within and close to the SPD and its youth branch, the JUSOS. By and large, these self-styled progressive internationalists endorsed the dependency school argument about U.S. imperialism.[17] The political importance of the JUSOS was often exaggerated, but as factional squabbling within the SPD intensified during the late 1970s and the neutralist movement grew in West Germany generally, this group gained ground in local SPD organizations and became especially vocal in expressing its opposition to U.S. policy in Central America. Its influence increased when the SPD lost power in 1982. Thereafter, the dynamic of opposition, the retirement or fading out of moderate leaders, and the strategy (adopted with Brandt's encouragement) of seeking to develop relations with the Greens and other representatives of the "new politics" heightened its importance.

Drawing the latter two schools of thought together

about Third World (and Central American) issues was a shared set of principles. The first was the primacy of the doctrine of nonintervention in "the internal affairs of another people."[18] The second was a common belief in the "third way" between communism and capitalism. This position was strongly reminiscent of the views held by SPD leader Kurt Schumacher after World War II, and it also echoed arguments that dated to the 1920s and 1930s. The third was a common emphasis on social justice themes and their relevance to international society. Such views were, of course, part of the more general Social Democratic legacy, but both "internationalist" schools felt they were the more appropriate custodians of this tradition.

Behind the SPD's discovery of the Third World in the 1970s lay both economic and political imperatives. The West German economy had expanded vigorously during the preceding two decades. Its dynamic growth was fueled by the capacity to develop markets and to generate exports. By 1978, indeed, the value of exports had come to represent nearly 30 percent of the gross national product (GNP).[19] The bulk of this trade has been with the EC and the United States. Increasingly, however, West Germany sought markets and investment opportunities in Third World countries. Another consideration, which became dramatically relevant after the post-1973 oil crisis, was the need to secure access to raw material supplies. West Germany had scant natural resources and, unlike England and France, had neither former colonies nor historically privileged relations with Third World countries upon which to rely.

This economic imperative sensitized West German (and SPD) foreign policy makers to the Third World's importance. How did Central America fit into this scheme of things? What balance was there between economic and political interest in this region? Here, of course, a sense of proportion is important. Certainly, Central America's relevance in purely economic terms was neither direct nor primary. West German trade and investment with Latin America was not centered in this region. Rather, its focus was in Argentina, Brazil, Mexico, and Venezuela.[20] Even if Central America hardly mattered in this regard, the region was relevant to West German economic strategy in Latin America and in the Third World generally. Central America was a symbol, a negative example of how the industrialized world (and, in particular, the United States) should not deal with the Third World. By focusing on the very evident mistakes that the United States had made in the region, the case was, in effect, being made to Third World elites about the Federal Republic's desirability as a partner.

Political factors were much more important than economic considerations, however, in explaining the SPD's engagement with Central American issues. As occurred in other European countries, the September 1973 overthrow of Chilean President Salvador Allende had focused the Social Democrats' attention on Latin America. In the wake of the coup, the SPD (like the SAP) had played a crucial role in resettling and providing support for numerous Chilean refugees in Western Europe. The subsequent success of the Iberian transitions to democracy encouraged the SPD to envision an even greater role for itself in Latin America.

Other circumstances provided additional impetus to Social Democratic efforts. During the 1970s, Latin America was a continent in transition. Authoritarian regimes and elites predominated in many countries, but public protest was also on the rise. The United States, reeling under the impact of the defeat in the Vietnam War and the constitutional crisis provoked by Watergate, appeared ready to accept a diminished role in Latin America. The SPD and especially its more "internationalist" wing led by Brandt was ready – indeed, eager – to increase its political engagement in the region.[21] Already in 1976 Brandt had organized a meeting in Caracas (Venezuela) at which European Socialist leaders met with representatives from various Latin American parties. Of the European contingent, the SPD was the most assiduous in following up these contacts, using both the Friedrich Ebert Stiftung and the SI as its primary vehicles for establishing links to the Latin Americans. By the time the Central American crisis exploded in the late 1970s (closely following the July 1979 Sandinista victory, a full-scale guerrilla war erupted in El Salvador), the SPD had already become deeply engaged, providing political and organizational support to the FSLN in Nicaragua and to Guillermo Ungo's MNR in El Salvador.[22] These initiatives had brought the Social Democrats into conflict even with the Third World-sensitive Carter administration. The advent of Ronald Reagan in January 1981 brought a much sharper confrontation with the United States and a correspondingly greater effort by the SPD to differentiate its policies from those of the United States.

It was not just external circumstances or developments that led to SPD engagement in Central America, however. Important domestic reasons also impelled the Social Democrats in this direction. The incorporation of the "successor generation" into Social Democratic ranks brought both an effort to revive a more class-based ideology and a greater sensibility to demands of the ecology and peace movements. How to deal with these movements became an even more pressing question after the March 1983 parliamentary elections, when the Green Party gained representation in the Bundestag. The Social Democratic perspective on Central American issues mixed conviction with clearly tactical considerations. No doubt many party militants doubted the wisdom of and disagreed with U.S. policy in the region. Neither was there any question that U.S. policy in Central America rivaled disarmament and deployment of tactical nuclear weapons as issues that stirred public passions, especially among the Greens and on the SPD's left wing. From this perspective, Central America served as an *ersatzweises Aktionsfeld*, a substitute field of action that offered the SPD an arena in which it could reaffirm its leftist credentials.[23] Similar to engagement with the peace movement, such a strategy sought to lure Green voters back into the SPD fold and broaden the basis for eventual national collaboration with the Green Party.

The Central American Policy of the SPD

The SPD was involved early in the unfolding crisis in Central America and the Caribbean. Beginning in the mid-1970s, the party and especially those individuals who rallied around Willy Brandt in his dual role as SPD chairman and SI president had directed their gaze toward the region. SPD and Friedrich Ebert Stiftung activists were the principal organizers of the 1976 Caracas meeting, and they provided the bulk of manpower and other resources for subsequent follow-up efforts. The most visible efforts were the creation of the SI's Latin America Committee in 1977 and the organization of a 1978 conference on "Processes of Democratization in Latin America and the Iberian Peninsula," hosted by Mário Soares and the Portuguese Socialist Party (PSP).

In pursuing these efforts, the SPD targeted three groups in the region: first, the historic stalwarts of democratic reformism – Venezuela's Democratic Action (AD) and Costa Rica's National Liberation Party (PLN). These parties had well-established organizations and traditions of regional solidarity. Their links to the SPD and European Social Democracy reached back to the 1950s and 1960s through their involvement in the International Confederation of Free Trade Unions (in which the West German Social Democratic trade union, the DGB, played a key role) as well as their participation in cooperative enterprises with the Ebert Stiftung. The latter established its first Latin American training center (CEDAL) just outside of San José (Costa Rica) in 1963; the Stiftung's Latin American journal *Nueva Sociedad* was published in Caracas.

A second SPD target was Mexico's Institutional Revolutionary Party (PRI). Heir to one of Latin America's longest revolutionary traditions, the PRI indulged in a much more nationalist and radical rhetoric than the AD or the PLN. Its ideology blended populism and nationalism into a formula for one-party authoritarian rule. Despite its questionable commitment to democratic socialism, the PRI invited the West German Social Democrats' attention: Mexico was evidently interested in gaining room to maneuver vis-à-vis the United States, and the PRI had extensive links with many smaller, nationalist or radical revolutionary movements in the region.[24]

Often avowedly Marxist-Leninist, aligned with Havana, and the recipients of training as well as support from Cuba, these movements constituted the third and most controversial SPD target in the 1970s. A number of these parties had been invited to the 1978 Lisbon conference; through the Friedrich Ebert Stiftung and informally through the SI, the SPD pursued its contacts with them. Especially significant in this context were the links that the Social Democrats forged with the Nicaraguan FSLN. By late 1978, the Sandinistas were receiving direct assistance from the SPD, and the facilities at CEDAL had been transformed into a school for preparing their members to assume the reins of government. A less intense but similar pattern of SPD engagement and support was evident in its relations with several other parties, including the New Jewel Movement (in power after an April 1979 coup in Grenada) and the MNR in El Salvador.

Like others in the French and Spanish Socialist parties, many SPD leaders welcomed the July 1979 Sandinista victory, believing that it augured a fundamental and positive realignment in Central American politics. More than other European Socialists, however, Brandt and his associates believed that they had played a special role in helping the FSLN come to power and thus had special access to and influence with the Sandinistas. Undoubtedly, this belief reassured them and other more moderate elements in the SPD (including some of the "Atlanticists" close to Schmidt and Apel) who, nevertheless, had serious qualms about the political and ideological allegiances of top FSLN leaders. For others, the more romantically inclined, for whom tropical revolutions provided exotic social laboratories, this concern was rather less pressing, and solidarity with Nicaragua knew few boundaries.

Whatever different sensibilities may be said to have existed within the SPD leadership in 1979, they were still subdued; the momentum, on the other hand, clearly favored an activist policy. On the heels of the Sandinista victory, there followed an expansion of SPD activities and strong expressions of support for the FSLN and other revolutionary movements in the region. The Ebert Stiftung opened an office in Managua, and within the SI, Willy Brandt asked Felipe González to head the Committee for the Defense of the Nicaraguan Revolution.

Following soon after Nicaragua, El Salvador became the other point of crisis in Central America and as such also attracted the Social Democrats' attention. In October 1979, a group of reformist officers had overthrown the conservative military government, installing in its place a revolutionary junta. One of its members was Guillermo Ungo, leader of the MNR. Frustrated by the intransigence of an army that refused to negotiate with the guerrillas and fearful of becoming merely a stooge for the traditional *oligarquía*, Ungo abandoned the junta in January 1980, throwing his lot with the FMLN guerrilla coalition. Coincidentally, his erstwhile colleague (they had run together and lost in the fraudulent 1972 election) and now rival, José Napoleón Duarte—leader of the Christian Democratic Party (PDC)—joined the junta. He promised to implement his own broadly reformist program that included a far-reaching agrarian reform. Both men, it should be said, had strong democratic instincts, and it has been the tragedy of El Salvador that each, hostage in his own way to extremist elements in society, could not work with the other. Whatever the case, Ungo's decision settled the issue for Brandt and other SPD leaders, as well as other members of the European Social Democratic family, who now came out squarely in support of the insurgents.

By this time, El Salvador had assumed center stage in SPD deliberations over Central America. Brandt and SI Secretary General Bernt Carlsson issued a congratulatory telegram on the occasion of the FMLN's January 1981 "final offensive," and even the SPD Presidium released a similar statement expressing its "solidarity" with the guerrillas.[25] Later the same year, Brandt and other party leaders expressed their strong support for the Franco-Mexican initiative that, in recognizing a "state of belligerency" in El Salvador, afforded equal status to both the Duarte government and the insurgents.[26] Having staked out these positions, SPD leaders were undoubtedly not surprised by the sharp reaction it provoked in the newly installed Reagan administration.[27] But if this was the case, what is less clear is how, at the same time, the Social Democrats could have supposed that the United States government would have taken up their oft-repeated offers to have the SI "mediate" in El Salvador.

The unequivocal and engaged posture embraced by party leaders (especially Brandt and the party's left wing) toward Central American issues contrasted with the more restrained position adopted by the SPD-led West German government through 1982. Here, Helmut Schmidt's political views and the exigencies of coalition government with the FDP had an important impact. Shortly after Somoza's overthrow, it is true, the Schmidt government had prepared an aid package for the new Sandinista government, and West Germany suspended approximately $14 million in development aid to El Salvador in 1980 because the safety of German administrators in the country could not be guaranteed. Neither of these decisions was made with the kind of enthusiasm and sense of purpose found among those close to Brandt and the SPD's left wing. For one thing, Schmidt represented the more "Atlanticist" wing of the party, and he strongly believed in the need to maintain a close U.S.-German relationship. Moreover, although he viewed the development of a West German presence in the Third World as important, Schmidt had a much less "political" agenda on this issue than Brandt, who preferred the international arena. Less dismissive of U.S. concerns about expanded Soviet influence in the Third World than others in the SPD, Schmidt was nevertheless not very eager to become involved in Central American issues. Asked once for his opinion of the crisis there, he laconically replied:

> It is a regional crisis with factors connected with the Cold War. Soviet influence in Cuba and Cuban influence in Central America should not be underestimated. But I do not really want to become involved in that question. I have too many problems to become involved in other people's.[28]

Given his institutional position as chancellor (and his own high popularity with the electorate), Schmidt was also somewhat insulated from party pressures, a circumstance reinforced toward the end of his mandate by the increasingly strident criticisms that he encountered in his own party.

The other circumstance that contributed to the government's restraint was the membership of the FDP in the ruling coalition. With 10.6 percent of the vote in the 1980 Bundestag election, the FDP was a crucial swing party and a necessary ally for the Social Democrats. Its views and in particular those of its leader, Foreign Minister Hans-Dietrich Genscher, had to be considered. From Schmidt's point of view, in any case, this situation would not have been entirely undesirable because it allowed him to counterbalance pressures from within his own party. A case in point was the official cabinet statement on El Salvador issued in early 1981 (which contrasted sharply in tone with the ones issued by the SPD and the SI), wherein the West German government refused to take sides in the conflict, saying there were "respectable democratic forces" on both sides.[29] The FDP was also active in seeking renewal of development aid to El Salvador. On this question, however, the opposition of SPD member and Economic Cooperation Minister Rainer Offergeld was too strong.[30] The ban prevailed through late 1983, when the Bundestag approved the new CDU-FDP government's aid package to El Salvador.[31]

After 1982, however, the SPD was no longer encumbered by governmental responsibilities. Neither did its left wing have to contend with the looming figure of Schmidt the chancellor. Within SPD councils, the Left was now increasingly powerful, and its representatives – two prominent examples were Oskar Lafontaine and Erhard Eppler – assumed important positions in the leadership. The result was a more progressive tone for the Social Democratic alternative in domestic and foreign policy. Along with overtures to the Green Party and the peace movement, there were party-to-party exchanges with a number of Eastern European Communist parties, most prominently with the East German Socialist Unity Party (SED) and the Hungarian Socialist Workers' Party (SWP).

These initiatives, it should be noted, were themselves not unconnected to generational changes taking place within the SPD leadership and to the battle being waged over the succession. After leaving the chancellorship, Schmidt had withdrawn from an active role in the party and would not run for his seat in the 1987 election. No clearer illustration of just how far his star had eclipsed within the party he had led could be cited than an article that appeared in the official SPD weekly *Vorwärts* in 1986.[32] It linked Rosa Luxemburg's murder during the *Spartacist* uprising (1918) first to the atrocities committed at Auschwitz and Dachau and then to the suicides of several members of the Baader-Meinhof group while in jail. Responsible for this trail of blood was the ruling class and its agents, "the Eberts and the Scheidemans, the Lebers and the Schmidts."[33] On the other hand, Brandt, who had gained a new lease on political life in the late 1970s and early 1980s, would also one day have to pass from the scene. Brandt's efforts to groom Oskar Lafontaine as his successor backfired, weakening him (he would resign as party chairman in 1987 after an embarrassing incident when he tried to appoint a Greek national to be SPD spokeswoman) and contributing to further factional infighting.

As the opposition, the Social Democrats had fewer constraints in dealing with Central American issues. This situation could not have been entirely satisfactory, however, because it also meant that the SPD's opinions would be accorded less weight by the Reagan administration. A paradoxical situation thus developed during the 1980s. On the one hand, there was little question that, more than any preceding U.S. government, the Reagan administration focused more attention on the European Social Democratic movement (and, particularly, the SPD) as well as on efforts to have these parties temper their criticisms of U.S. policy. On the other hand, at no time since the end of World War II had the chasm, the sense of mutual distrust and ignorance, between the United States and the SPD been so great as during this period, when the more ideological elements on both sides were perversely joined by a stereotypical form of reasoning. The result was that, even on many issues where common ground might have been found, compromise became impossible.

As they had been when the SPD was in power, El Salvador and Nicaragua retained their salience for the party once it entered the opposition. Accordingly, they offer useful prisms through which to analyze the post-1982 evolution and diversity in SPD thinking about Central American issues. El Salvador provides the most clear-cut case in this respect. Brandt and the Social Democratic left wing had early on been unambiguous in their support for the guerrillas, and in late 1980 and early 1981, they had set the tone for the party as a whole. Even at this time, however, there had been evidence of a slightly less categorical view within the party. A joint appeal was issued in May 1981 by prominent FDP and SPD parliamentarians, including Horst Ehmke and Karsten Voigt (whose views on foreign policy fell somewhere between Schmidt's "Atlanticist" wing and the "Euro-internationalist" group gathered around Brandt), as well as AnneMarie Renger (who was close to Schmidt). The appeal called for a "dialogue between democrats" in El Salvador and criticized "extremists and fanatics" on both sides.[34]

These more moderate views toward El Salvador gained influence within the SPD as time passed. Of course, they did not sway the party's left wing, which remained adamantly critical of Duarte and U.S. policy. Solidarity committees, which were often organized by the German Communist Party but included rank-and-file Social Democrats and JUSOS, collected money for the guerrillas.[35] Brandt, too, did not easily or, at least, publicly change his position on El Salvador. On the occasion of the March 1983 legislative elections (won by Duarte and the Christian Democrats), he drafted an SI Presidium statement that referred to the "so-called elections" there.[36] It is true that those elections had been held under difficult conditions: "Death squads" remained mercilessly active, and Ungo's MNR had chosen for this (and other) reasons not to participate. Even so, however, it would be difficult to deny that the election, which gave the Christian Democrats an absolute majority in the National Assembly, represented an important development. Symptomatically, Hans Koschnik, later to become chairman of the SPD's International Committee, urged the Social Democrats on this occasion to stop playing schoolmaster.[37]

Duarte's victory in the June 1984 Salvadorean presidential elections encouraged a further shift in Social Democratic perspectives. The party had opposed the Kohl government's decision to seek aid for El Salvador, but in a development that could not have been imagined a year or two before, Horst Ehmke and other SPD leaders (as well as Friedrich Ebert Stiftung representatives) nevertheless met with Duarte when he visited Bonn in July 1984.[38] Whatever opinion Social Democratic leaders may have had about the Salvadorean, by this time most of them recognized that he and his party could be neither ignored nor dismissed, all the more because he was the recognized linchpin in the Reagan administration's strategy toward El Salvador. The result was a blend of confidence-building measures combined with a strategic decision to focus most of their attention on neighboring Nicaragua.

Although they ceaselessly called for a "political" solution to the Salvadorean conflict, the Social Democrats saw little prospect of a negotiated settlement without a broader, regional agreement, and for this reason, they greatly encouraged the Contadora process. Despite this "minimalist" perspective, there was an active Social Democratic effort to build bridges to the Salvadorean Christian Democrats and to find a formula that would allow the return of MNR and other leftist opposition leaders to the country. Here, the indefatigable traveler, Hans Jürgen Wischnewski, played an important, if not always successful, role.[39] A frequent visitor to El Salvador, he helped negotiate the release of Duarte's kidnapped daughter with the FMLN in late 1985. Nearly two years later, as a member of an SI delegation, Wischnewski accompanied Guillermo Ungo when, following the August 1987 Esquipulas II Agreement, the latter made his first trip back to El Salvador in November 1987.[40]

Nicaragua was the second and – as the 1980s wore on – the more significant Central American point of reference for the SPD. As in El Salvador, events in Nicaragua soon dissipated many Social Democrats' initial enthusiasm for the Nicaraguan Revolution and, as the crisis in that country and throughout the region worsened, these events led to nuanced differences within the party. Here, it should be stressed, the cleavage line was not between those who supported U.S. policy in Central America and those who did not. Indeed, few within the SPD fell into the former category. Where disagreements existed, they reflected instead differences over how West Germany and the Social Democratic movement should relate to the United States and to revolutionary movements in the Third World.

The more radical perspective – similar to the "progressive internationalist" approach described earlier – viewed Nicaraguan events primarily through the lens of "solidarity." Its advocates were unwavering in their support of the Sandinistas. They regarded the FSLN as an exemplary national liberation movement whose efforts to ensure Nicaragua's independence and right to self-determination as well as to create the foundations for a socialist society were indeed worthy of support. For them, whatever restrictions had been imposed on civil and political rights or whatever harassment of the civilian opposition had occurred were lamentable but, in the final analysis, understandable, given that – as they argued – U.S. support for the contras had created the war-like conditions in Nicaragua.

Although advocates of this progressive perspective did not command an active majority within the SPD leadership or, certainly, among its electorate, they were often able to influence the agenda on Nicaraguan issues within party councils. This occurred, for example, in early November 1984 when the party Presidium issued a resolution on the Nicaraguan presidential elections. Drafted by Uwe Holtz and Peter Von Oertzen, the document was conspicuously contentious. Making only the most general allusion to possible human rights violations in Nicaragua, it did not even obliquely criticize the role of Sandinista hardliners who, by refusing to accept an SPD proposal for an extension in the deadline for negotiations between the FSLN and Arturo Cruz at the SI's Rio de Janeiro meeting, had helped to torpedo his participation in the presidential elections. By contrast, the resolution sharply criticized U.S. pressure on Nicaragua and blamed the Reagan administration for putting the Sandinistas in the position of having to choose, so it said, between capitulating to the contras or abandoning their regime's pluralistic nature.[41]

Among the most important reasons for the influence of the progressive perspective within the SPD leadership was the role its proponents played in maintaining the Social Democrats' contacts with activists from the peace movement and the myriad solidarity groups that had proliferated in the Federal Republic during the 1980s. These groups drew their members from the JUSOS, the SPD, the Communist Party (DKP), and some unions and churches. Their network collected money and organized volunteer "brigades" that went to Nicaragua to help with coffee harvests or to provide medical assistance.[42] Active at the municipal and *Land* (provincial) levels, these solidarity groups encouraged various governmental entities (in Hesse, Nuremberg, and Wiesbaden, among others) to establish their own development aid programs and technical exchanges with Nicaragua.[43] Because a number of these volunteers were killed or kidnapped by the contras, their activities both fueled domestic West German controversy and strengthened the hand of the Social Democratic left wing in party circles.[44]

Not all SPD leaders shared this perspective of unreflective solidarity and identification with the FSLN and the Nicaraguan Revolution. Although a strong tradition of party discipline and unhappiness with the Reagan administration's policy toward Nicaragua (not to mention an unwillingness to be seen bowing to domestic and foreign pressure) contributed to a contrary image, there was actually some criticism of Sandinista behavior.

Those who adopted a more critical perspective toward the Sandinista project were divided into a number of distinct orientations. One group included Hans Apel (still in the Presidium in 1986) and the remnants of the Schmidt wing of the party which represented a small minority in the leadership. They had little sympathy either for the Sandinistas or for their SPD colleagues who supported the FSLN and participated with Communists and other radicals in the Latin American "solidarity" groups. In November 1984, on the occasion of nationwide rallies in support of Nicaragua (Brandt spoke at the meeting in Bonn), Hans Apel decried as a *Schweinerei* ("pigheadedness") the Berlin Social Democrats' decision to join in a rally whose organizers included Communist front organizations.[45]

In a second category were several other national SPD leaders (Johannes Rau, Hans-Jochen Vogel, and Hans-Jürgen Wischnewski). Even if they criticized U.S. policy toward Nicaragua, nevertheless they considered it important, not least for the sake of West German and European security, to remain on good terms with the United States with which they shared democratic values.[46]

Of the three, it was Wischnewski who had the most visible profile on Central America and played the leading role in SPD discussions with the Sandinistas. A man of pragmatic orientation and one of the few top SPD leaders with a working-class background, Wischnewski was an indefatigable negotiator.[47] As often as not, his meetings with FSLN representatives were, to borrow a phrase, "frank and cordial." Although there is little doubt that he alternatively lobbied and pressed the Sandinistas (as occurred during a trip to Managua in early 1984 when he urged the FSLN to hold free and open elections or, later, during the unsuccessful negotiations with Bayardo Arce at the Rio de Janiero SI meeting), he usually eschewed public criticism of their behavior, preferring to resort to the Aesopic "original project" formula. His view was that open lines of communication had to be maintained and nothing done to provide ammunition to the Reagan administration.[48]

By early 1986, in any case, Wischnewski had begun to deliver his message to the Sandinistas more publicly. On the one hand, he repeated his opposition to U.S. support for the contras and insisted that Nicaragua was not a Communist state.[49] On the other, he criticized the fusion of party and state there ("These structures are moving in a direction which is not democratic") and cautioned the FSLN that its promises were not sufficient either to ensure internal reconciliation or to end the civil war.[50]

Among representatives of the SPD's left wing, there also was evidence of growing criticism toward the FSLN during the 1980s. Here, however, two positions can be identified. The first was represented by Hans-Ulrich Klose, former mayor of Hamburg and more recently (1987) appointed SPD treasurer. The second consisted of the "Euro-internationalist" group, of which Willy Brandt was the premier exponent.

Klose expressed the misgivings of those on the Left who were troubled by the Nicaraguan government's record on human and civil rights. His credentials could not be contested. Forced from his post as mayor by Helmut Schmidt, who resented his opposition to nuclear energy, he had also been an early Sandinista supporter. Upon his

return from a trip to Central America in December 1985,
however, he surprised and outraged many of his colleagues
(they questioned both his knowledge and motives) when he
presented a report that criticized the Nicaraguan government for its human rights violations.[51] Publication of
Klose's report was doubly embarrassing for the SPD because it occurred just when the party was embroiled in a
controversy over the effort by its Cologne federation to ex-
pel one of its members, a university professor named Mar-
tin Kreile, for having written a book sharply critical of both
the Sandinistas and SPD policy toward Central America.[52]

Willy Brandt brought another perspective to these issues and, more broadly, to the debate over Nicaragua. His
was, of course, a more "authoritative" point of view. On the
one hand, undoubtedly the tone of Brandt's statements had
changed considerably by the mid-1980s. The euphoria
about the prospects for change in Central America was re-
placed by oblique criticisms of the Sandinistas and an insistence on their adherence to the "original project." Usually
these comments were rendered inconsequential by the
much sharper barbs directed at the Reagan administration.
Brandt was not, as some maintain, being manipulated by
the FSLN *comandantes*. He was no novice. Few could
doubt his political acumen or the breadth of his information
about Nicaraguan events. Brandt also had a very definite
belief about his role in the theater of world politics. In West
German politics, Brandt considered himself to be a point of
reference for the younger generation of leftists whom he
hoped ultimately to attract to the SPD standard.

What differentiated Brandt from Klose, for example,
was his carefully articulated international strategy. Eurona-
tionalism, the dream of a Europe autonomous from both
superpowers, provided the positive drive behind this vision
and led Brandt toward engagement with the Third World.
But there was also a more negative thrust to his ideas. It
led him away from a concern with the internal consequences
of authoritarian rule, be it in Poland or Nicaragua. Here the
impetus came from his views about the superpowers and

their imperial ambitions. Brandt's protestations to the contrary, there can be little doubt that, at the very least, he viewed the United States and the Soviet Union as morally and functionally equivalent.[53] Whatever reasons Brandt may have had for developing this perspective (and perhaps the pointed exchanges with the Reagan administration had contributed to it), the result was often the subordination of concerns about internal Nicaraguan developments (such as human rights violations) to the imperative of limiting U.S. influence in the region.[54]

Conclusion

The subtle but unmistakable shift in the SPD's position toward Nicaragua had an important impact on its role and influence in the region. Party spokesmen now routinely balanced their criticism of U.S. policy with warnings to the Sandinistas that SPD support was neither unconditional nor automatic. Although the SPD would still hesitate before demanding that the Nicaraguan government release Lino Hernández Trigueros (head of the Independent Human Rights Commission, who had been arrested as he sought to participate in a human rights demonstration in Managua in August 1987), there was nevertheless mounting evidence of a more evenhanded SPD approach toward the Nicaraguan government.[55] The SPD attended the February 1987 meeting hosted by the PSOE (mentioned earlier in chapter 2) and, along with the other European Socialist party representatives in attendance, took FSLN leaders to task. Holding out the possibility of improved relations and continued support, those in attendance (among whom was Brandt) called on the FSLN to change course by lifting the state of emergency, reopening the newspaper *La Prensa*, and improving relations with Costa Rica.[56] On this latter issue, the SPD echoed the demand, voiced by the other parties, that Nicaragua withdraw its complaint against Costa Rica before the International Court of Justice.[57] Further attesting to the changed SPD approach was its involvement only a few months later in an incident that led the Nicaraguan government to recall its ambassador to Bonn for having openly chastised the SPD and the SI for their "unfounded" criticism of the revolution.[58]

Conclusion

This monograph has reviewed the evolving perspectives and activities of several major European Socialist and Social Democratic parties regarding Central America. Although some of these parties (most notably, the SPD) had been active in the region since the 1960s, it was only after the July 1979 overthrow of Anastasio Somoza in Nicaragua and the onset of civil war in El Salvador, and as part of a broader effort to establish a presence in the Third World, that European Socialist engagement in Central America visibly expanded. Using a wide array of instruments (party-to-party links, government-sponsored loans and credits, and aid funneled through foundations and trade unions), these parties provided important support and afforded international legitimacy to many left-wing groups and movements throughout the region.

As indicated in the material presented in the case-study chapters, the reasons for and the modalities of European Socialist involvement in Central American issues varied from party to party and country to country. Nonetheless, there were certain common denominators that impelled their engagement during the 1970s and early 1980s. Perhaps the most important were the changes associated with the shift from bipolarity to multipolarity in the international system. If competition between the United States and the Soviet Union remained an important point of reference, this rivalry, as well as the equilibrium attained in the superpower relationship during the 1970s, also encouraged other actors in the international system—both national and transnational—to seek ways of sidestepping the logic of superpower hegemony. A parallel and related development was the emergence of economic power blocs in other regions of the world, a development that led Western Europe and Japan (to cite only the most prominent examples) to intensify their competition with the United States in the search for market and investment opportunities in the Third World.

Accompanying these changes in the economic and political balance of power was a shift in the international role and self-perception of Western European and Latin American actors. The decline of U.S. hegemony, of U.S. imperial will and capacity, coincided with a revival of nationalist sentiment in both regions, which encouraged governments and political groups there to extend the range and scope of their international links—generally and with each other. Pursuit of the European–Latin American connection made particular sense in this context. An attractive European model had developed in the years since World War II, combining political pluralism and democracy with dynamic economic growth and the existence of an ample welfare state. The model appealed to many Latin American elites who wished for a "Western" connection and imprimatur but also wanted to enhance their independence from the United States. There was no direct nor immediate threat to Latin American sovereignty posed by the European "offer," and what assistance the latter provided—precisely because it would not be of a military nature—was unlikely to provoke a sharp U.S. response.

The 1970s had witnessed the first tentative steps toward articulating a common European position on international questions. With the EC's increased economic clout, sentiment grew in favor of greater political activism. During this period, too, the international activities of political transnational organizations expanded on the Continent. Their first major international engagement had come in Spain and Portugal, where many European parties, foundations, and trade unions (not to mention the respective political Internationals) had played an important role during the transitions to democracy.

Emboldened by this experience and eager to extend their links elsewhere in the world, the principal European political families turned their attention to Latin (and Central) America during the 1970s, transporting to the region not only their vast array of networks but also a political style that emphasized transnational and regional cooperation. This "offer" was especially relevant in Central America where the historic weakness of civil society had been aggravated and brought into sharp relief by a profound economic and social crisis during the 1970s. Engendered by a sharp decline in the world-market price of agricultural goods and a coincident explosion in the numbers and demands of the urban population, the crisis helped to undermine and overwhelm the political system. The ensuing polarization and intensified cycle of violence encouraged political groups throughout the region to seek external sources of support, laying the groundwork for involvement by extracontinental actors. The more radical groups considered the European connection the formula for avoiding clearcut identification with the Soviet Union or Cuba. The more moderate groups were eager for external contacts as counterweights to reinforce their domestic legitimacy, provide organizational and financial support, and enhance their leverage vis-à-vis more radical or hardline elements.

Of those Europeans who stepped into the Central American breach in the 1970s, none did so with a higher profile and greater sense of purpose than representatives of the European Socialist movement. The intellectual architects of this involvement—Willy Brandt and his colleagues, Olof Palme and Bruno Kreisky—considered the region an arena where European socialism could both reassert its historic identity as an anticapitalist force and make a positive contribution to the democratization of the region. At the same time, through their criticism of and competition with the United States, these parties could also affirm their nationalist credentials. While partaking of the more general European desire to assert an international presence (especially on Third World issues and disarmament questions) and to gain maneuverability vis-à-vis the two superpowers, the Socialists brought their own international traditions to the region as well as an advocacy of a "third way" between capitalism and communism.

Our review of European Socialist initiatives in Central America reveals that this engagement has passed through three phases. The first phase (1978–1981) was one of unbridled optimism and intense involvement, during which the conviction generally prevailed that revolutionary change in the region was both necessary and desirable. Solidarity with the Sandinistas in Nicaragua and the FMLN-FDR coalition in El Salvador was at its zenith. Conversely, criticism of the United States and its policies in the region (notably enough, this began when the Carter administration was still in office and lasted into the first year of the Reagan presidency) was at its most strident. During this period, the highest profile on Central American issues belonged to the left wing of the SPD, whose leader, Willy Brandt, was both party chairman and president of the Socialist International. From this latter position, in particular, he pressed for active solidarity with "progressive" movements in the region.

The other highly visible actor was the French Socialist government under President François Mitterrand. It burst on the Central American scene in mid- and late 1981 after signing a declaration with Mexico (which recognized a "state of belligerency" in El Salvador) and deciding to sell arms to the Nicaraguan government. The Spanish PSOE was also highly visible during this period, particularly through Felipe González's frequent trips to the region and his position as head of the SI Committee for the Defense of the Nicaraguan Revolution. Of the Socialist leaders who became interested in Central America during this period, it was he (and the Portuguese Socialist, Mário Soares) who was most cautious about alignment with revolutionary movements in the region.

The second phase of European Socialist engagement (1982–1986) was one of modified perspectives and reduced activism. There was growing disenchantment with Sandinista restrictions on civil and political rights as well as with Nicaragua's growing alignment with the Soviet bloc. A change was also evident toward El Salvador, where most European Socialists now neither anticipated nor desired a guerrilla victory. Instead they focused on finding a way to negotiate a settlement in the civil war.

There were several reasons for these shifts in perspective. For one, the Reagan administration had come into office ready to make of Central America a test case for its foreign policy. The October 1983 invasion of Grenada and the administration's success in gaining congressional funding for the contras further diminished what hopes the European Socialists might have had for influencing events in the region. Moreover, as the conflicts in Central America assumed an international dimension and thereby began to touch on more vital aspects of the U.S.-European relationship, the more pragmatic elements in the Socialist parties began to reassert themselves, urging diminished engagement as well as a less confrontational posture vis-à-vis the United States. Related to this development was the conclusion shared by many moderates in these parties that, however much they might disagree with the Reagan administration's policies in the region, the European Socialist movement had not been quite careful enough in selecting its Central American interlocutors during the 1970s. The retrenchment was, in any case, most evident in France and Spain where the Socialists had governmental responsibilities and concluded early on that confrontation with the United States over its Central American policies would be of little benefit. Their foreign policy agendas contained oth-

er, more important items for which cooperation with the
United States would be necessary. Yet another reason for
French and Spanish Socialist caution was the reaction,
sharply negative in the first case and flatly unenthusiastic
in the other, which their major diplomatic incursions (in
1981 and 1983) elicited. A more cautious and restrained
approach was also evident in the case of the West German
Social Democrats, although here the dialectics of opposition and the SPD strategy of courting the Greens gave
some added weight to the party's left wing.

Renewed activism and intensified engagement in support of negotiations set the tone for European Socialist
involvement during a third phase (1986-1989). A number of
circumstances encouraged the reactivation of their efforts
in the region. For one, the Reagan administration was in a
much weaker position than it had been in the early 1980s.
The Democratic Party had captured control of the U.S. Sen-
ate in the 1986 congressional elections, and the Iran-contra
scandal had further undermined the administration's policies. There was also a new and more fluid situation in Central America, and it encouraged the nations of the region to
support the regional peace initiatives associated with the
Arias Plan and the August 1987 Esquipulas II Agreement.
In El Salvador, government and guerrillas were locked in a
stalemate. In Nicaragua, the contras had proven their ability to wage successful economic war but had nevertheless
failed to defeat the FSLN militarily. At the same time, economic and social chaos threatened to engulf the Sandinista
government. These circumstances and the existence of the
regional forum created by the Esquipulas II Agreement
offered the European Socialists and, in particular, the Spanish PSOE and West German SPD (who were by now their
most active representatives in the region) a new opportunity for engagement.

Unlike a decade or so earlier, when they had been un-
abashedly partisan and supportive of revolutionary change,
the European Socialists now emphasized their credentials
as "honest brokers," eager to encourage negotiations and

ready to coordinate their efforts with regional actors. Reagan administration policies and, particularly, its efforts to secure funds for the contras were still sharply criticized, but there was also support for Vinicio Cerezo and the still unsteady transition in Guatemala as well as a much more evenhanded approach toward José Napoleón Duarte and his Christian Democratic Party in El Salvador. Despite occasional reminders of past ambivalence (as when the SPD hesitated in August 1987 before demanding that the Nicaraguan government release Lino Hernández Trigueros, head of the Independent Human Rights Commission, who had been arrested in August 1987, or when Spanish Vice Prime Minister Alfonso Guerra praised Nicaragua for having gone farthest in implementing the Esquipulas II Accords), there were also many fewer punches pulled with respect to the Sandinistas or the guerrillas in El Salvador. FSLN leaders were alternately cajoled and warned about developments in Nicaragua. In El Salvador, the European Socialist strategy was to encourage Guillermo Ungo and his colleagues in the FDR to resume civic life in their country, with the hope that this might ultimately weaken extremist sectors on both Right and Left who wished for a continuation of armed struggle, thereby contributing to a negotiated settlement.

And what of the future? What conclusions may be drawn from the European Socialist experience in Central America over the past fifteen years? A first inclination would be to stress the limits, the obstacles, to a continued or enhanced European Socialist presence in the region. A decade ago interest was strong and optimism marked. Today Central America is no longer on the international front burner. Despite renewed Socialist activism after 1986, there is little evidence that either individual European countries (where the Socialists rule or have significant influence) or the European Community are willing to bridge the gap between rhetoric and action by providing substantial development assistance for the region or according its exports preferential treatment. At the head of the line, in this respect, are those African, Mediterranean, and Asian countries whose bond with Western Europe (France and West Germany, in particular) are much stronger. There is manifest weariness (not to say frustration) with the problems and demands of the region. There has been a distinct waning of the earlier rosy expectations when it was assumed that profound changes were destined to sweep the isthmus and what mattered was how to link up with those forces presumed to be in the ascendant.

To mention the setbacks and reconsiderations of the past decade or to emphasize the obstacles to a deeper economic relationship between Western Europe and Central America should not cause one to underestimate the significance and longer-term implications of European Socialist involvement in Central America, however. One need not agree with all aspects of their policy in the region (in the opinion of this author the European Socialists made a serious mistake in Nicaragua and El Salvador in the late 1970s and early 1980s) to recognize the positive contribution that their efforts have made to the development and institutionalization of a democratic Left in Costa Rica, Guatemala, and Honduras. Moreover, it is also true that only he who abstains completely from engagement avoids mistakes.

The record of the past decade suggests that the PSOE and the SPD are much more likely than the PS to pursue an activist course in Central America. Both the SPD and PSOE have focused on institution building and cadre training, establishing a broad network of contacts throughout the region. Currently the Social Democrats, who have the Friedrich Ebert Stiftung at their disposal and whose leaders have been very active in the Socialist International as well, have a decided edge on their Spanish counterparts. The SPD has a strong and well-defined sense of internationalist mission as well as the organizational capacity to implement a long-term political strategy.

The Spanish Socialists also have an incentive to remain active in Central America. Continued engagement in the region would not only reaffirm the PSOE's own domestic accomplishments and identity; it would also allow party leaders to claim for Spain a special role in the European Community as Central America's privileged interlocutor. Within Central America, too, there will be an effort to maintain the European Socialist "connection." Whatever the final outcome of negotiations currently under way in the region, diverse actors in the region have had a taste of international solidarity (from Christian Democratic and Liberal as well as Socialist sources), and they are unlikely to relinquish it. The very weakness of nation-states in the region and their vulnerability to external forces suggests that transnational groups and organizations will remain a significant part of the Central American political landscape in the coming years.

European Socialist engagement in Central America has had and will continue to have important implications for the broader U.S.-European relationship. During the past decade, Central American issues have been at the core of bitter controversies between the Reagan administration and various European Socialist and Social Democratic parties. The virulence of these disputes has been tempered more recently. Limited resources, a modified perspective about the desirability of revolutionary change in the region, a process of internal reequilibration that strengthened the hand of more moderate elements, and a reconsideration of the benefits to be derived from direct confrontation with the United States led the European Socialists away from their original partisan engagement and toward a more cautious relationship with the Sandinistas and other revolutionary movements in Central America.

The Reagan administration position also changed. The initial emphasis it had placed on security and strategic considerations as well as military instruments were certainly not abandoned after 1982 (attested to by continued support for the contras), but in the later years of its mandate, the themes of economic development and democratization for the region now assumed much greater prominence. No less relevant here was the Reagan administration's diminished political capacity regarding Central America (especially after 1986), a development whose most visible expression could be found in the protagonism of Central American nations as exhibited by the Arias Plan and Esquipulas II initiatives. As the end of the Reagan presidency approached, this trend became even more pronounced.

At the end of the 1980s, Central America is no longer on the front line of divergences between the Reagan administration and the European Socialists. Whether it will be resurrected as such is difficult, if not impossible, to predict. It is also important to realize, however, that the debate between the Reagan administration and the European Socialists was not merely about Central America, nor about how to deal with revolutionary change in the Third World and how to interpret Soviet capacities and intentions there. The argument also reflected a broader set of problems provoked by an ongoing reequilibration of the Atlantic relationship. Whether it finds expression in Central America or elsewhere, whether a Democratic or Republican administration governs in Washington, whether Mikhail Gorbachev's much vaunted "new thinking" dramatically alters the main lines of Soviet foreign policy toward Western Europe and the Third World, resurgent European nationalism is here to stay. The European Socialists have both partaken of this nationalism and contributed to it, while also affirming their more specific identity through the rediscovery of historic themes – such as pacifism and neutralism – and renewed advocacy of a "third way" between capitalism and communism. These are ideas that should continue to animate European Socialist international activities over the next decade; as such, they are likely to be central to the Western European debate about the nature of the transatlantic relationship.

Notes

Chapter 1

1. Hereafter the terms "Socialist" and "Social Democratic" are used interchangeably whenever reference is made to the pan-European or international movement. For individual parties, on the other hand, the appellations used by each party will be used. The formal names of the parties with which we shall be centrally concerned in this monograph are France's Parti Socialiste (Socialist Party), Spain's Partido Socialista Obrero Español (Spanish Socialist Workers' Party), and West Germany's Sozialdemokratische Partei Deutschlands (Social Democratic Party).

2. For an excellent introduction to the international Social Democratic movement, see Julius Braunthal, *History of the International* (London: Frederick Praeger Inc., 1967), volumes 1 (1864–1914) and 2 (1914–1943). Also Arthur Rosenberg, *Democracy and Socialism* (Boston: Beacon Press, 1965), and G. D. H. Cole, *Socialist Thought* (London: Macmillan, 1953), Parts 1 and 2.

3. For an overview of the development and policies of the Communist International, see Franz Borkenau, *The Communist International* (London: Faber and Faber, 1938).

4. Even so, the lesson was not learned immediately and everywhere, as became evident in the case of the Italian Socialist Party (PSI) which, under the leadership of Pietro Nenni, systematically pursued joint action with the Italian Communists (PCI) well into the 1950s. One result was a split in the PSI in 1948, and the creation of the Partito Social Democratico Italiano (PSDI).

102

On Italian foreign policy in the 1940s and early 1950s, see F. Roy Willis, *Italy Chooses Europe* (New York: Oxford University Press, 1971). For a discussion of the Italian Communist Party (PCI) that includes more general references to the Italian Left, Donald L. M. Blackmer, *Unity in Diversity: Italian Communism and the Communist World* (Cambridge, Mass.: The M.I.T. Press, 1968).

5. For an assessment of the "liberal socialism" this produced, see William David Graf, *The German Left since 1945 – Socialism and Social Democracy in the German Federal Republic* (Cambridge, England: The Oleander Press, 1976), 197–212.

6. On this point, see Gordon D. Drummond, *The German Social Democrats in Opposition 1949-1960: The Case against Rearmament* (Norman, Okla.: University of Oklahoma Press, 1982), and Wolfgang Hanrieder, *West German Foreign Policy, 1949-63* (Stanford, Calif.: Stanford University Press, 1967).

7. For a statement of this position, see Daniel Bell, *The End of Ideology* (New York: The Free Press, 1965). On the "catchall" party, Otto Kirchheimer's influential essay in Myron Weiner and Joseph LaPalombara, eds., *Political Parties and Political Development* (Princeton, N.J.: Princeton University Press, 1966).

8. Ronald Inglehart, *The Silent Revolution: Changing Values and Political Styles among Western Publics* (Princeton, N.J.: Princeton University Press, 1977) presents the classic argument about shifts occurring in the value priorities of a significant sector of West European publics.

9. Stephen Szabo, ed., *The Successor Generation: International Perspectives of Postwar Europeans* (London: Butterworths and Co., 1983), presents a general and useful review.

10. On the evolution of the SPD, see Gerard Braunthal, *The West German Social Democrats 1969-1982: Profile of a Party in Power* (Boulder, Colo.: Westview Press, 1983). Chapter 5 (pp. 85–105) discusses the Jungsozialisten or JUSOS.

11. Frank Wilson's "The French Left in the Fifth Republic" in William Andrews and Stanley Hoffman, eds., *The Fifth Republic at Twenty* (Albany, N.Y.: State University of New York Press, 1981) provides an excellent overview.

12. For a general discussion, see Gerhard Kiersch's "Konflikt, Kooperation und strukturelle Dominanz: Frankreichs Sozialisten und die SPD," in Kiersch and Reimund Seidelmann, eds., *Eurosozialismus: Die demokratische Alternative* (Cologne: Europäische Verlagsanstalt, 1979).

13. On this point, see Miles Kahler, *Decolonization in Britain*

and France (Princeton, N.J.: Princeton University Press, 1984), 161–230.

14. The latter sentiment found eloquent expression in the so-called Brandt Report (formally entitled *North-South: A Programme for Survival*, 1980), and in the Report of the Socialist International Committee on Economic Policy published as *Global Challenge – From Crisis to Cooperation: Breaking the North-South Stalemate* (1985).

15. Willy Brandt, Lecture at St. Antony's College (Oxford University) on May 27, 1980.

16. Cole, *Socialist Thought*, Part 2, p. 895.

17. Braunthal, *History of the Socialist International* (vol. 2), 552. Appendix 5 contains the Manifesto of the Third Congress of the Labour and Socialist International (August 5–11, 1928).

18. Ibid., 266.

19. A number of books and articles have dealt with these themes. Among the most useful: A. Glenn Mower, Jr., *The European Community and Latin America: A Case Study in Global Expansion* (Westport, Conn.: Greenwood Press, 1982); Bernard Lietaer, *Europe and Latin America and the Multinationals: A Positive Sum Game for the Exchange of Raw Materials and Technology in the 1980s* (New York: Praeger, 1980); Georges Landau and Harvey Summ, eds., *The European Community Enlargement and Latin America* (Westport, Conn.: Greenwood Press, 1986); Gustavo Lagos, ed., *Las Relaciones entre América Latina, Estados Unidos y Europa Occidental* (Santiago: Instituto de Estudios Internacionales de la Universidad de Chile, 1980); and Riordan Roett and Wolf Grabendorff, eds., *Latin America, Western Europe and the US: Reevaluating the Atlantic Triangle* (New York: Praeger, 1985). Of the articles, several by Wolf Grabendorff have been especially helpful. See his "Las Relaciones entre América Latina y Europa Occidental: Actores Nacionales y Transnacionales, Objetivos y Expectativas," *Foro Internacional* (Mexico) 23, no. 4 (Autumn 1982): 625–637, and "The Central American Crisis and Western Europe: Perceptions and Reactions" (Research Institute of the Friedrich Ebert Stiftung, 1982). Others include Simon Serfaty, "Atlantic Fantasies," in Robert W. Tucker and Linda Wrigley, eds., *The Atlantic Alliance and Its Critics* (New York: Praeger, 1983), and Simon Serfaty, *The United States, Western Europe and the Third World* (Washington, D.C.: Center for Strategic and International Studies, 1980).

20. In the case of Spain, for example, this was not a difficult

task; after the loss of its empire (the Spanish-American War, 1898, represented the final, bitter nail in the process), that country turned inward, consumed by virulent political quarrels that ended in the Civil War (1936-1939). British and German economic and political presence in Latin America declined more slowly, with British investments being larger than total U.S. investment in Latin America until the Great Depression.

21. For a general discussion, Esperanza Durán, *European Interests and Latin America* (London: Routledge & Kegan Paul Ltd., 1985).

22. For a general discussion, see Serfaty, *The United States, Western Europe and the Third World*. On West Germany, see Michael Kreile, "West Germany: The Dynamics of Expansion," in *International Organization* 31, no. 4 (Autumn 1977): 635-667, and Wolfram F. Hanrieder and Graeme P. Auton, *The Foreign Policies of West Germany, France and Britain*, (Englewood Cliffs, N.J.: Prentice Hall Inc., 1980), 3-96. On France, Lawrence G. Franko and Sherry Stephenson, *French Export Behavior in Third World Markets* (Washington, D.C.: Center for Strategic and International Studies, 1981).

23. European trade ties with Latin America developed neither as rapidly nor as strongly as advocates of the "new" relationship had hoped. Preferential ties European countries had with former colonies and protectorates (the Lomé and Yaoundé conventions), growing EC protectionism, the incorporation of Spain and Portugal into the Community, and the United States' continued importance as a market and source of imports for Latin America worked against it. Economic relations did expand, however. Europe became the second largest market for Latin American exports (see "Las Relaciones Externas de América Latina en el Umbral de los Años Ochenta" in *Comercio Exterior* 29, no. 6 [June 1979]: 673-684). And in the late 1970s France, West Germany, Italy, and Great Britain became the largest arms suppliers to the region, accounting between 1975 and 1979 for an estimated $2.2 billion in arms sales, compared with $725 million for the United States in the same period (*Miami Herald*, November 29, 1982). The flow of European investment was also significant: through the late 1970s, Latin America absorbed more direct European investment than any other region in the developing world. See Blanca Muñiz, "EEC-Latin America: A Relationship to be Defined," *Journal of Common Market Studies* 29, no. 1 (September 1980): 55-64 (at 63). Even though Spain's exports to Latin

America represented only 10.6 percent of its total exports, by the late 1970s Spanish investments totaled nearly $800 million (54 percent of total Spanish direct investment overseas), and Spanish banks had lent over $10 billion to Argentina, Brazil, Mexico, Venezuela, and Cuba. See Daniel Szabo, "Direct Investment and Financial Flows," in Landau and Summ, *The European Community Enlargement*, 229–241; and *Financial Times* (London), November 10, 1981. For its part, West Germany also developed a strong relationship with the first four of those countries. They accounted for over $3 billion (or 70 percent) of German exports to the region. Statistical Office of the European Community, *Analytical Tables of Foreign Trade* [NIMEXE] (Luxembourg, 1976–   ), 117. More notably, through 1979, 47 percent of German foreign investment in developing countries was in Latin America. Cited in Peter Hermes, "Aspects and Perspectives of German-Latin American Policy," *Europa-Archiv* (Bonn) 24, no. 14 (1979): 421–430. Also see *Politik der Partner* (German Development Ministry, 1981), 134.

24. For a historical review of these activities, see Michael Löwy, "Trayectoria de la Internacional Socialista en América Latina," *Cuadernos Políticos* (Mexico), no. 29 (July–September 1981): 36–45; Felicity Williams, *La Internacional Socialista y América Latina* (Mexico: Universidad Autónoma Metropolitana, 1984), 163–230; and María Isabel Allende, *La Internacional Socialista y América Latina: Pasado y Presente de una Relación Difícil* (Santiago: Instituto Latinoamericano de Estudios Transnacionales, 1983), 73–120.

25. On the points contained in this paragraph, see Carlos Morales Abarzua, *La Internacional Socialista en América Latina y el Caribe* (Mexico: Editorial Patria Grande, 1981), 122–125, and Allende, *La Internacional Socialista y América Latina*, 130–133.

26. The first letter in the exchange came from Brandt in February 1972, and the correspondence continued into early 1975. For a French language version, see Willy Brandt, Bruno Kreisky, and Olof Palme, *La Social-Démocratie et l'Avenir* (Paris: Editions Gallimard, 1976).

27. The argument was phrased in general terms but, as we shall discuss later in this monograph, a call for "Germano-Swedish-Austrian" collaboration was not far from the surface. Ibid., 247 and 252.

28. Ibid., 249.

29. These figures are estimates derived from numerous con-

versations in Madrid, Lisbon, and Bonn with knowledgeable observers and participants. The SPD was not the only Socialist or Social Democratic party that gave financial support to the Spanish and Portuguese Socialists – only the most important.

Brandt took an almost paternal approach toward Felipe González. Helmut Schmidt intervened on several occasions with the Spanish government in support of González and the PSOE. On one occasion, it was to ensure that González would be granted a passport to travel to the SPD Congress in Mannheim in November 1975. Pressures were also forthcoming on the Spanish government to permit the Socialist General Workers' Union (UGT) to hold its congress in Madrid in May 1976 and then to permit the PSOE to hold its own congress in December 1976. SPD *Bundestag* deputy Hans Matthöffer was also affectionately known as the "deputy from Barcelona."

Newspaper references to aid from the Swedish SAP may be found in *Informaciones* (Madrid), December 30, 1975, and *ABC* (Madrid), April 4, 1976. The second item claims 22 million Spanish *pesetas* had been transferred between December 1975 and March 1976.

European assistance to the Portuguese Socialists was also significant. See Tad Szulc, "Lisbon and Washington: Behind Portugal's Revolution," *Foreign Policy* 21 (Winter 1975–1976): 3–26. As in Spain, alongside organizational and financial support, it consisted of prominent European Socialist personalities descending on Lisbon to join in the PS electoral campaigns. The SPD-led West German government played a key role in putting together an emergency aid package made available to Portugal by the EC in mid-1975 – on condition that the country retain a parliamentary regime.

Chapter 2

1. For a discussion of Spanish foreign policy objectives and concerns, see my essay "Rei(g)ning in Spain," in *Foreign Policy* 51 (Summer 1983): 101–117.

2. *XXVII Congreso del Partido Socialista Obrero Español* (Barcelona: Editorial Avance, 1977), 136.

3. Ibid., 136 and 332.

4. *ABC* (Madrid), November 5, 1978.

5. *El País* (Madrid), August 10, 1978.

6. González interview with the *Frankfurter Allgemeine Zeitung* (Frankfurt), December 1, 1984.

7. Elena Flores, "A Modo de Introducción," *Caminos de la Democracia* (Madrid: Ediciones Fundación Pablo Iglesias, 1984), 63. Flores has been responsible for the PSOE's international relations and in 1983 was a precandidate for the post of Socialist International secretary general.

8. *El País*, December 12, 1983.

9. *ABC* (Madrid), January 25, 1981. See also the later article by Joaquín Leguina, Socialist head of the Madrid Autonomous government, in *Diario16* (Madrid), March 9, 1984, in which he reflected on how much his views had changed since the early 1970s. Even so, the *El Socialista* correspondent had written a nearly panegyric article when reporting, without irony, on the meeting of "Intellectuals against Repression" in Havana in late 1981. See *El Socialista*, September 23–29, 1981, pp. 46–47. For an excellent review of Hispano-Cuban relations, see Joaquín Roy, "Percepciones de España en el Nuevo Mundo: El Caso de Cuba," a paper delivered at the Latin American Studies Association national meeting in Boston, October 22–25, 1986. Also Juan del Aguila, "España y el Conflicto entre Cuba y Estados Unidos" in Instituto de Cooperación Iberoamericana, *Realidades y Posibilidades de las Relaciones entre España y América en los Ochenta* (Madrid: Ediciones Cultura Hispánica, 1986), 7–16.

10. The conditions were nonintegration in NATO's military wing, a prohibition against nuclear weapons on Spanish soil, and a reduction in the number of U.S. troops stationed in Spain. Subsequent emphasis on the latter demand complicated U.S.-Spanish relations, leading to drawn-out base negotiations whose result was an agreement in early 1988 to withdraw the 401st Air Squadron from Torrejón over the next three years. *El País* (Madrid), January 14, 1988.

11. *Socialist Affairs* (London), no. 3 (May–June 1981), 120. This journal is the Socialist International's official organ.

12. *El Socialista* (Madrid), December 3–9, 1980, p. 49.

13. Ibid., December 17–23, 1980, p. 47 and October 22–28, 1980, p. 47.

14. *Socialist International Press Release*, no. 12/82, April 2, 1982.

15. *El Socialista*, March 24–30, 1982, p. 32 for the quotation.

A different perspective could be gained from reading the articles on April 14–20, 1982, pp. 40–41 and May 5–11, 1983, p. 46.

16. The quotation is from a González interview with *Crítica* (Panama), October 25, 1982.

17. *El País*, December 4, 1982.

18. Ibid., February 13, 1983.

19. See Felipe González's speech as cited in *Actividades, Textos y Documentos de la Política Exterior Española—1983* (Madrid: Oficina de Información Diplomática, 1984), 187.

20. Quoted by the EFE News Agency on March 3, 1983 and translated in *Foreign Broadcast Information Service—Western Europe* (hereafter FBIS–WE), March 4, 1983, p. N1.

21. Quoted in *ABC*, April 21, 1983.

22. *Washington Post* (Washington, D.C.), July 11, 1983.

23. For a brief description of the effort, see Jean Grugel, "Spain's Socialist Government and Central American Dilemmas," *International Affairs* (London), no. 4 (1987): 610–611.

24. *Unomasuno*, May 28, 1983.

25. Material in this paragraph is drawn from the sources here mentioned. If there was anyone in the Nicaraguan government who knew the details of the ETA connection, it was Borge. Perhaps the other Sandinista leaders believed that he should take the heat and try to convince the Spanish to the contrary. Borge, of course, insisted that there was "no organic or political link with that organization known as ETA." *El País*, September 22, 1983. The Costa Rican government, headed by Luis Alberto Monge, hardly agreed and sent Vice President Alberto Fait to Madrid to present its case. *La Vanguardia*, October 29, 1983. On ETA activities in Central America, see the Spanish Ministry of the Interior report leaked to *El País*, January 13, 1984. On the ETA-FSLN link, see the testimony by Foreign Minister Morán and the former Spanish ambassador to Managua, Mariano Baselga Mantecón, before the Foreign Relations Commission of the Congress of Deputies. *Diario de Sesiones del Congreso de Diputados* (1984), IIda. Legislatura (no. 40), 6 and (no. 131), 4314–4318.

26. See the *Report of the Meeting of the Secret Regional Caucus* (January 6–7, 1983) drafted by the New Jewel Movement's representative, Chris de Riggs. Document 100446 in the National Archives (Washington, D.C.). Published in *Grenada Documents: An Overview and Selection* (Washington, D.C.: Government Printing Office, 1984).

27. Conversations in Madrid (June 1984).

28. SPD leaders Wischnewski and Brandt presented this initiative in conjunction with Carlos Andrés Perez.

29. *El Pais*, November 7, 1984.

30. *Latin America Weekly Report*, May 17, 1985, pp. 6–7. The credit lines, closed in mid-March 1985, were reopened in June 1985. *El Pais*, June 29, 1985.

31. *Cambio16*, August 13, 1984, p. 40.

32. See *New York Times*, December 25, 1985, p. A3.

33. See the coverage in *El Pais*, January 9 and 12–17, 1986.

34. She was the author of a controversial document, leaked in early 1988, criticizing the Castro regime for its human rights violations. "From the human rights point of view, Cuba's position is very weak and its record leaves much to be desired," it declared. See *ABC*, February 25, 1988.

35. On the organization of ICI, see the *Real Decreto* 359/ 1981 (February 5, 1981) and various reports presented at the Seminar on International Cooperation: Institutional and Administrative Aspects, Madrid, June 1983. Although its budget has grown since 1982, ICI still spends the bulk of its resources (approximately 60 percent) on administrative costs in Madrid. *El Pais*, September 17, 1983 and March 12, 1984.

36. In attendance at this meeting were representatives from the French PS (International Secretary Louis Le Pensec), the Swedish SAP (Undersecretary of State Pierre Schori), SPD (Willy Brandt and Hans-Jürgen Wischnewski), and the PSOE (Vice Prime Minister Alfonso Guerra and Elena Flores). For a newspaper account, see *Ya*, February 18, 1987.

37. The crucial margin was provided by those who abstained rather than vote "for," but more especially "against," the government's proposal.

38. Significantly, Pierre Schori, who represented the Swedish SAP and was among the strongest supporters that the Sandinistas had in the Socialist International, spoke first and detailed the European concerns. For his part, González did not meet with the FSLN representatives, Bayardo Arce.

39. *El Pais*, April 9 and 10, 1987.

40. Ibid., October 3, 1987. Broken off because of guerrilla intransigence, these negotiations were renewed in late February 1988.

41. Ibid., March 12 and 13, 1988.

42. Ibid., November 28, 1987.

43. In Western Europe, Ortega visited Italy, Spain, Norway, and Sweden.

44. *El País*, March 8 and 11, 1988. The FSLN newspaper *Barricada* (January 28, 1988) had cited Spanish approval of the idea but made no reference to any conditions.

Chapter 3

1. Dominique Moïsi, "Mitterrand's Foreign Policy: The Limits of Continuity," *Foreign Affairs* 60, no. 2 (Winter 1981/1982): 347–357, and Michael Harrison and Simon Serfaty, *A Socialist France and Western Security*, Occasional Papers in International Affairs (Washington, D.C. and Bologna, Italy: The Johns Hopkins Foreign Policy Institute, 1981).

2. Patrice Buffotot, "Le parti socialiste et l'internationale socialiste (1944–1969)," in Hugues Portelli, ed., *L'Internationale socialiste* (Paris: Éditions Ouvrières, 1983), 93.

3. *Le projet socialiste – Pour la France des années 80* (Paris: Club Socialiste du Livre, 1980), 341.

4. Jean-Pierre Cot, *A l'Épreuve du Pouvoir – Le tiers-mondisme pour quoi faire?* (Paris: Éditions du Seuil, 1984), 16.

5. For this phrase, see the heading in *Pour le socialisme: Le livre des assises du socialisme* (Paris: Lutter/Stock 2, 1974), 42. Party Secretary Lionel Jospin also edited a book on the Third World. See *Les socialistes et le Tiers Monde* (Paris: Éditions Berger-Levrault, 1977). More generally, the discussion in Jean Touscouz, "Le parti socialiste français et la coopération avec le Tiers-Monde," *Politique étrangère* (Paris) 46, no. 6 (1981): 875–889. Also Richard Gombin, "Le parti socialiste et la politique étrangère – Le programme de 1972," *Politique étrangère* 42, no. 2 (1977): 199–212.

6. Threads of the argument about politics and economics can be found in numerous publications. Among the most relevant, see *Pour le socialisme; Le projet socialiste;* and François Mitterrand, *Ici et maintenant: Conversations avec Guy Claisse* (Paris: Librairie Artheme Fayard, 1980). The discussions in Michael Harrison, "A Socialist Foreign Policy for France?" *Orbis* 19, no. 4 (Winter 1976): 1471–1496 and David Yost's review essay in *Armed*

Forces and Society 8, no. 2 (Winter 1982): 334–345, are also very useful on this point.

For a fascinating review on the consumerist culture, see Denis Lacorne et al., *L'Amérique dans les têtes — Un siècle de fascination et d'aversions* (Paris: Editorial Hachette, 1986).

7. *Changer la vie — Programme de gouvernement du Parti Socialiste* (Paris: Éditions Flammarion, 1972), 198.

8. *Le projet socialiste*, 340. The text was prepared after the PS lost the March 1978 parliamentary elections. A few pages later, there followed the almost obligatory disclaimer: "Remaining within the Atlantic Alliance cannot signify an acquiescence to American strategy [p. 348]." See also, François Mitterrand, *Politique, textes et discours 1938–1981* (Paris: Éditions Marabout, 1984), 257.

9. For a translated text, see FBIS — WE, January 23, 1983, pp. J1–4.

10. See, for example, the statement of Minister of Finance Jacques Delors to a United Nations-sponsored conference on Least Developed Countries in September 1981 in *Le Monde* (September 5, 1981), and the memorandum circulated by the French government at the Cancún summit quoted in *Le Monde* (October 22, 1981). Also interesting is the Mitterrand speech to the September 1981 meeting of the United Nations as reprinted in *Statements from France* (Embassy of France) 81/77, and Claude Cheysson's speech to the United Nations General Assembly in the same month (ibid., 81/79).

11. See Régis Debray's remarks in 1974 as reproduced in *Pour le socialisme*, 123–126.

12. Franz-Olivier Giesbert, *François Mitterrand, ou la tentation de l'histoire* (Paris: Éditions du Seuil, 1977), 312.

13. *Le Monde*, April 23, 1981.

14. Ibid., March 31, 1981.

15. Guy Hermet, "L'Amérique Centrale vaut mieux que de beaux gestes," *Politique internationale*, no. 21 (Fall 1983), 143–152.

16. *Le Monde*, October 22, 1981.

17. Ibid., August 30, 1981.

18. *Latin America World Report* (London), January 15, 1982, p. 4, and *Washington Post*, January 9, 1982. One analyst reports that the initiative had been initially "vetoed by the Foreign Minis-

try, (but) it was revived and awarded the presidential imprimatur through a cabal involving the Socialist Party international affairs bureau, the inclinations of Elysée expert Régis Debray, and the influence of the president's wife." Michael Harrison, "Mitterrand's France in the Atlantic System: A Foreign Policy of Accommodation," *Political Science Quarterly* 99, no. 2 (Summer 1984): 222.

19. *New York Times*, January 9, 1982.

20. *Le Point* (Paris), March 31, 1982, p. 99.

21. *El País*, September 4, 1981, and *Washington Post*, September 3, 1981. For a biting analysis of Mitterrand's policy, see Michel Tatu, "La position française: Les difficultés d'être un bon 'latino,'" *Politique étrangère*, no. 2 (1982), 319–324.

22. *Financial Times* (London), March 10, 1982.

23. *Foreign Broadcast Information Service (Latin America)*, August 5, 1983, p. F1, quoting a Reuters dispatch dated August 4, 1983.

24. Reuters News Agency dispatch, November 23, 1984.

25. *Latin American Monitor*, October 1–31, 1984, p. 109.

26. *Le Monde*, July 14, 1982. In an interview with the FSLN's newspaper *Barricada* (July 13, 1982), Mitterrand pointedly noted: "The Sandinista revolution must also remain faithful to its principles; at least this is my wish, and I am sure that the Sandinista leaders have the same hope."

27. *L'Express* (Paris), 47. In an October 1, 1984 interview with *Libération* (Paris), Cheysson was critical about the timing and organization of the elections. The Franco-Nicaraguan friendship group in the National Assembly (which included Socialists) did send observers.

28. *Washington Post*, April 15, 1984. For an apparent text of the letter, see *Barricada* (Managua), April 4, 1984.

29. *L'Unité* (Paris), April 2, 1982.

30. *Le Monde*, February 27, 1983.

31. *Latin America Weekly Report*, July 27, 1984, p. 2, provided an overview of the Duarte trip to France, Great Britain, and West Germany.

32. For material on France's African policy and the Cot resignation, see *Le Point* (Paris), December 13, 1982, pp. 60–61, and May 17, 1982, pp. 90–94; *Le Quotidien de Paris*, June 7 and 10, 1982; *Washington Post*, December 18, 1984. For interesting general accounts of the infighting, see Philippe Bauchard, *La guerre*

des deux roses (Paris: Éditions Grasset, 1986) and Thierry Pfister, *La vie quotidienne à matignon au temps de l'Union de la Gauche* (Paris: Librairie Hachette, 1985).

33. Christopher Dickey, "Central America: From Quagmire to Cauldron," *Foreign Affairs* (America and the World, 1983), 681–682.

34. *Latin America Weekly Report*, April 26, 1985, p. 10 and May 10, 1985, pp. 4–5. Also *Le Point*, April 15, 1985, p. 41.

35. First, PS International Secretary Jacques Huntzinger traveled to Havana in February 1982 in a visit reciprocated by Cuban Vice Prime Minister Carlos Rafael Rodríguez's trip to Paris in May. Minister of Culture Jack Lang, a vociferous critic of U.S. cultural imperialism and a representative of the party's left wing, went to Havana in July 1982. Among his statements was one insisting both Cuba and France "believ(ed) in man and reject the international dictatorship of a standardized and industrialized monoculture." *Le Monde*, July 28, 1982. The Cuban Minister of Culture Armando Hart subsequently (in March 1983) went to Paris. His trip came several months after Cuba had released two well-known dissidents (Armando Valladares and Andrés Vargas Gómez) from jail. These gestures were made to obtain an official invitation for Fidel Castro to visit Paris. The visit did not materialize, at least in part because of the French government's acute embarrassment over Cuban mistreatment of another dissident (Ricardo Bofill), who had sought asylum in the French embassy in April 1983. Promised freedom from harassment if he left the embassy, Bofill was arrested five months later.

36. *Latin American Monitor*, May–June 1985, p. 167.

37. For a discussion of this role and Mitterrand's style, see Marie Claude Smouts, "The External Policy of François Mitterrand," *International Affairs* (London), Spring 1983, pp. 156–158. Also the analysis in the Harrison article in *Political Science Quarterly* (220–226) cited earlier.

38. Harrison, *Mitterrand's France in the Atlantic System*, 222.

39. About him, see the article in *New York Times*, May 3, 1984, and the interview in *Le Nouvel Observateur* (Paris), October 26, 1984, pp. 50–51.

40. For a brief biography, see *Le Monde*, April 21, 1985.

41. For an overview of PS international activities and statements, see *Rapports d'activité du secrétariat international et déc-*

larations de politique internationale du Parti Socialiste (*Octobre 85-Avril 87*) presented at the Lille Congress in April 1987.

42. The quotation is from Cheysson's reply to a written question in the National Assembly. FBIS—WE, March 3, 1983, p. K2.

Chapter 4

1. For a useful historical overview, see Braunthal, *The West German Social Democrats—1969-1982*.

2. See Table 16 in Tilman Evers, "Die westdeutsche Sozialdemokratie in Lateinamerika: Offensive oder Flucht nach vorne?" in Forschungs- und Dokumentationszentrum Chile-Lateinamerika (ed.), *Sozialdemokratie in Lateinamerika* (Berlin, 1982), 71.

3. In one sense, the Social Democratic-led governments were building on the commitment to European unification that had been at the core of Christian Democratic Chancellor Konrad Adenauer's strategy from the 1940s. His idea had been for a strong West German commitment to both the European Community and NATO. By the 1970s, there was a perceptible if still small current of opinion within the SPD that linked the "Europeanization of Europe" (to borrow a phrase from Peter Bender's provocative analysis in "The Superpower Squeeze," *Foreign Policy*, no. 63 [Winter 1986-1987]: 98-113) to disengagement from the Atlantic Alliance and equidistance from the blocs.

4. For sharply critical views of this development, see several of the essays in Jürgen Maruhn and Manfred Wilke, eds., *Wohin tribet die SPD? Wende oder Kontinuität sozialdemokratischer Sicherheitspolitik* (Munich: Olzog Verlag, 1984).

5. For an analysis of West German opinion on security issues, see Peter Schmidt, "Public Opinion and Security Policy in the Federal Republic of Germany," *Orbis* 23, no. 4 (Winter 1985): 719-742.

6. Ferdinand Müller-Rommel, "Social Movements and the Greens: New Internal Politics in Germany," *European Journal of Political Research* 13, no. 1 (March 1985): 53-67.

7. For general and useful overviews, see Peter H. Merkl, "Pacifism in West Germany," *SAIS Review*, no. 4 (Summer 1982): 81-91, and Jeffrey Herf, "War, Peace, and the Intellectuals—The

West German Peace Movement," *International Security* 10, no. 4 (Spring 1986): 172–200.

8. The August 1987 joint SPD-SED statement contains a version of this argument. For its text, see the *Frankfurter Allgemeine Zeitung* (Frankfurt), August 28, 1987.

9. For example, Ernst Breit, chairman of the DGB, and Egon Bahr and Johannes Rau of the SPD *Vorstand* sit on the Board of Directors as do Peter Von Oertzen, Peter Glotz (until recently party secretary general), and Horst Ehmke. The analysis presented in this paragraph draws on written and oral source material. The interested reader is referred to several articles in the *Washington Post*, July 24, 1979, and September 1, 1980; the Ebert Stiftung annual reports (*Jahresberichte* 1977–1982); *Der Spiegel* (Hamburg), April 16, 1979; "History, Objectives and Work of the Friedrich Ebert Stiftung," a report delivered to the Caribbean Congress of Labor in January 1977; and the journal *Nueva Sociedad*.

10. *German Press Review* (New York), April 25, 1986, p. 5, and the *Antwort der Bundesregierung auf die Kleine Anfrage der Abgeordneten Schily, Suhr und der Fraktion DIE GRÜNEN* (*Drucksache*) 10/4652 – April 4, 1986. The exact amount of public moneys provided to the foundations and the specific projects they funded would not have been disclosed but for a parliamentary interpellation by the Greens.

11. Felicity Williams, *La Internacional Socialista y América Latina* (Mexico: Universidad Autónoma Metropolitana, 1984), 220–221.

12. The SPD and FES have maintained various contacts with the Cuban Communist Party (PCC). Following up an earlier meeting held in Bonn, the FES sponsored a colloquium on Politics in Western Europe in Havana in May 1985.

13. For a general analysis, see Serfaty, *The United States, Western Europe and the Third World*, 20–31. Policy statements to this effect abound. See Helmut Schmidt's address to the Bundestag in FBIS–WE, February 29, 1980, pp. J1–9, and Hans-Dietrich Genscher, "Toward an Overall Western Strategy for Peace, Freedom and Progress," *Foreign Affairs* 61, no. 1 (Fall 1982): 42–66.

14. As Peter Bender, a writer who is close to Brandt, has argued: "If the cause from which a third world war could arise is to be found in the dualism between the Americans and the Russians, then the first thing that has to be done is to reduce the

effectiveness of this dualism. Many parts of the world should remove themselves from the conflict of the superpowers or be removed from it. The Americans tend toward the globalization of their power struggle with Moscow, but for Europe the exact opposite is needed." *Das Ende des Ideologisches Zeitalters* (Berlin: Severin and Siedler Verlag, 1981), 194.

15. See also, Willy Brandt, "North-South Division," *Socialist Affairs*, nos. 3–4 (March/April 1979): 95–98; Uwe Holtz, "SPD and the New International Economic Order," in ibid., 48–50. Also interesting are a number of the speeches delivered to an SPD conference in September 1977 reprinted in *Forum SPD* (Fachtagung "Entwicklungspolitik der SPD" am. 1 und 2, September 1977, in Wiesbaden).

16. Egon Bahr, "From the perspective of the SPD: Towards a Consensus on Basic Development Policy," a speech delivered in Bad Godesberg on January 25, 1979.

17. See, for example, former JUSOS leader and currently Bundestag deputy Heidemarie Wieczorek-Zeul's statements about Latin America. In particular, her speech to the Asamblea Legislativa in Costa Rica reprinted in *Sozialdemokratischer Pressedienst* 37, no. 109 (June 11, 1982): 8–9, and her "15 Thesen zum Verhältnis EG-Lateinamerika und zu einer kohärenten Lateinamerika-Politik aus socialdemokratischer Sicht" (manuscript, 1982). The local Hessen-South branch of the SPD approved a statement in early 1981 that described the FDR as "the legitimate representative of the broad majority of people in El Salvador" and "condemn[ed] the efforts of the US government."

18. The phrase was contained in the 1959 *Grundsatzprogramm* approved at Bad Godesberg.

19. The figure was 28.8 percent for the Federal Republic of Germany, 18.4 percent for Japan, and 7.7 percent for the United States. Cited in the chapter by Manfred Mols entitled "The Latin American Connection" in Peter H. Merkl, ed., *West German Foreign Policy: Dilemmas and Directions* (Chicago: Council on Foreign Relations, 1982), 108.

20. Ibid., 107–108. Also Dieter W. Benecke et al., *The Relations between the Federal Republic of Germany and Latin America: Present Situation and Recommendations* (Bonn: Research Institute Friedrich Ebert Stiftung, 1985), 15–16. An excellent overview of German development strategy with respect to Latin America may be found in a special issue of the journal *Contribuciones para el Debate* devoted to cooperation between the Federal

Republic of Germany and Latin America. In particular, see Klaus Bodemer, "La política alemana para el desarrollo de América Latina—Sus fases, tendencias y perspectivas," *Contribuciones para el Debate* (Argentina), no. 1 (1986): 51–66.

21. On this point, see Willy Brandt, "Effective Solidarity," *Socialist Affairs* (London), nos. 11–12 (1979): 164–165, and Klaus Lindenberg, "Focus on Latin America—View from Bonn," ibid., nos. 9–10 (1979): 148–151.

22. For an exposition of Brandt's views, see his "Nuevas perspectivas para América Latina" in *Nueva Sociedad* (Caracas) (November–December 1979): 72–76.

23. The phrase is from Evers, "Die westdeutsche Sozialdemokratie in Lateinamerika," 59.

24. In October 1979, the PRI organized its own "regional" International, the *Conferencia Permanente de Partidos Políticos de América Latina* (COPPPAL). The organization brought together 23 "democratic, nationalist, socialist, and anti-imperialist groups." *La Vanguardia* (Barcelona), March 20, 1982.

25. For a general discussion, see articles in the *Frankfurter Allgemeine Zeitung*, February 2, 3, and 6, 1981.

26. IPS (West Germany) Press Dispatch, September 18, 1981.

27. The newly elected Reagan administration sent Assistant Secretary of State for European Affairs Lawrence Eagleburger to Western Europe in mid-February 1981 in an effort to rally support for U.S. policy toward Central America. Among the countries Eagleburger visited was West Germany, where he met with top government and party representatives, including SPD leaders. *Frankfurter Allgemeine Zeitung*, February 18, 1981. The importance that the incoming administration attached to Central America is well known. The Carter administration policy in Central America had become a major campaign issue in November 1980. Soon after Reagan assumed office, the U.S. State and Defense departments issued the *White Book on El Salvador* that stressed the Soviet-Cuban role in supporting the insurgency there, and a short time later, Secretary of State Alexander Haig, referring apparently to Cuba, warned that the United States was ready "to go to the source" in dealing with the El Salvador situation.

28. *Le Monde*, February 24, 1982.

29. *Frankfurter Allgemeine Zeitung*, February 5, 1981.

30. *Der Spiegel*, August 18, 1982, p. 16.

31. The new minister for economic cooperation, Jürgen Warnke of the Christian Social Union, had tried to release the funds in November 1982, but this action was blocked by Kohl and the CDU. See the Deutsche Presse Agentur (DPA) press dispatches from November 16 and December 6, 1982, as quoted in FBIS – WE, November 17, 1982, p. J6 and December 6, 1982, p. J4. Only after the Salvadorean Christian Democratic Party (PDC) had won an absolute majority in the National Assembly did the Kohl government move to resume the aid. The broad guidelines for this resumption were laid down during a July 1983 meeting with Duarte in Bonn. See FBIS – WE, July 12, 1983, p. J2.

32. *Vorwärts* (Bonn), April 5, 1986.

33. Schmidt wrote an angry letter to the SPD Presidium, and the party, of course, disclaimed the story. *Die Zeit* (Hamburg), April 23, 1986. SPD collaboration with Communists in the peace movement and in Central American "solidarity" groups provides another example of the "new" mood among certain sectors in the SPD.

34. *Frankfurter Rundschau*, May 23, 1981.

35. See *Der Spiegel*, December 12, 1983, pp. 88–89, for a lengthy article on these "solidarity committees."

36. *New York Times*, April 3, 1983.

37. Ibid.

38. Deutsche Presse Agentur, July 18, 1984. Having in effect "recognized" Duarte, the SPD called on him to lift the state of emergency, enter into a dialogue with the FMLN, and to combat the "death squads" more effectively.

39. An interesting glimpse into one of his trips (in May 1983) is provided by the "Bericht über die Reise des SPD-Präsidiumsmitglied Hans-Jürgen Wischnewski vom 9–25 Mai 1983 nach Mittelamerika und in die Karibik" (mimeo.).

40. *Frankfurter Rundschau*, November 21, 1987.

41. Ibid., November 3 and 5, 1984. Hans Apel, the former defense minister, refused to sign the resolution because it was too anti-American.

42. In an allusion to those who fought in Spain during the 1936–1939 civil war, they were referred to as *brigadistas*.

43. *Frankfurter Allgemeine Zeitung*, August 5 and 25, 1986.

44. See *New York Times*, September 17, 1986 for a general overview of the volunteers' activities. In June 1986, Hans-Jürgen Wischnewski helped negotiate the release of eight volunteers who had been held hostage for nearly four weeks by the contras.

45. *Frankfurter Allgemeine Zeitung*, November 1, 1984.

46. For a sense of intra-SPD differences, compare the interviews with Uwe Holtz and those with Johannes Rau and Hans-Jürgen Wischnewski in *Vorwärts*, April 7 and September 8, 1983, respectively.

47. Among the FSLN leaders, Wischnewski apparently had the best personal rapport with minister of the interior and reputed hardliner, Tomás Borge, who dubbed the West German *comandante*. *Vorwärts*, March 1, 1984. Also conversations in Bonn (June 1986) and Madrid (February 1988).

48. For an elaboration of this argument, see *Frankfurter Allgemeine Zeitung*, November 3, 1984.

49. Led by Wischnewski, the SPD *Fraktion* issued a public statement calling on the U.S. Congress not to appropriate any further aid to the contras. *Kölner Stadt-Anzeiger* (Cologne), March 6, 1986.

50. *Stuttgarter Zeitung* (Stuttgart), February 15, 1986.

51. See Hans-Ulrich Klose and Klaus-Henning Rosen's *Bericht über eine Informationsreise zur Lage der Menschenrechte in Zentralamerika (vom 23 November bis zum 8 Dezember 1985)*, issued on January 22, 1986. For a reply from the "progressive" sector, see Peter Von Oertzen's article in *Vorwärts*, February 22, 1986.

52. On this controversy, see *Die Zeit* (Hamburg), February 7, 1986, and the *Kölner Stadt-Anzeiger* (Cologne), June 14–15, 1986.

53. See his *Der organisierte Wahnsinn* (Cologne: Verlag Klepenhauer & Tisch, 1985), especially 134–138 and 191–205.

54. Disregarding the advice of U.S. Ambassador Arthur Burns, for example, President Reagan snubbed Brandt during his 1985 visit to the Federal Republic of Germany. He also refused to see Brandt when the former chancellor visited the United States.

55. *Frankfurter Allgemeine Zeitung*, August 21, 1987.

56. *Ya* (Madrid), February 18, 1987 carried a brief account of the meeting.

57. Agreement on this question was announced at the Socialist International Council's meeting in April 1987. *El País*, April 9 and 10, 1987.

58. See the report in the *Frankfurter Allgemeine Zeitung*, July 7, 1987.

Index